Inspiring Soccer Stories for Kids

The Legendary Tales of 12 Iconic Soccer Stars

Hayden Fox

© Copyright 2024 - All rights reserved.

The content contained within this book may not be reproduced, duplicated or transmitted without direct written permission from the author or the publisher.

Under no circumstances will any blame or legal responsibility be held against the publisher, or author, for any damages, reparation, or monetary loss due to the information contained within this book, either directly or indirectly.

Legal Notice:

This book is copyright protected. It is only for personal use. You cannot amend, distribute, sell, use, quote or paraphrase any part or the content within this book, without the consent of the author or publisher.

Disclaimer Notice:

Please note the information contained within this document is for educational and entertainment purposes only. All effort has been executed to present accurate, up to date, reliable, complete information. No warranties of any kind are declared or implied. Readers acknowledge that the author is not engaged in the rendering of legal, financial, medical or professional advice. The content within this book has been derived from various sources. Please consult a licensed professional before attempting any techniques outlined in this book.

By reading this document, the reader agrees that under no circumstances is the author responsible for any losses, direct or indirect, that are incurred as a result of the use of the information contained within this document, including, but not limited to, errors, omissions, or inaccuracies.

Claim your free gifts!

(My way of saying thank you for your support)

Simply visit **haydenfoxmedia.com** to receive the following:

- 10 Powerful Dinner Conversations To Create Amazing Kids

- 10 Magical Affirmations To Help Kids Become Unstoppable in Life

(you can also scan this QR code)

Table of Contents

Introduction 6

Chapter 1: Pele (1940 - 2022) 9

Chapter 2: President George Weah (1966 -) 23

Chapter 3: Mia Hamm (1972 -) 32

Chapter 4: David Beckham OBE (1975-) 42

Chapter 5: Didier Drogba (1978 -) 54

Chapter 6: Zlatan Ibrahimovic (1981 –) 64

Chapter 7: Christine Sinclair (1983 -) 74

Chapter 8: Marta (1986 -) 85

Chapter 9: Cristiano Ronaldo (1983 -) 96

Chapter 10: Lionel Messi (1987 -) 108

Chapter 11: Neymar (1992 -) 122

Chapter 12: Kylian Mbappe (1998 -) 132

Conclusion 142

Introduction

The famous Liverpool football manager Bill Shankley was famous for a famous quip, *"Some people believe football (soccer) is a matter of life and death, I am very disappointed with that attitude. I can assure you it is much, much more important than that."* This was actually a misquote (Jones, 2020), but perhaps because it rings true with so many people around the world, it is repeated frequently by fans.

The origins of soccer (or football as it is known in all other countries except for the U.S., Canada, Southern Africa, Japan, Australia, and the Pacific Islands) are still something we learn about every day. As it is such a simple pastime requiring so little, one can imagine how even ancient cavemen would have played a variation of the sport by kicking around stones or fruits in between two rocks or trees. It is then probably the greatest irony that it is exactly this way that many of the modern greats first learned to play.

Just about every continent has its own soccer origin story too. We have documented evidence of the Chinese playing a game called Kujo as early as 300 BCE, where two teams needed to get a ball into a net without using their hands. Ancient Greek art depicts humans playing Episkyros, where two teams would try to get the ball across their opponent's line using hands and feet. North America has its origin stories pertaining to the Aztec Empire. South American tribes tell of a game involving kicking a ball too, where the losers would often end up being sacrificed. Quite a scary thought, right?

The modern game of football is thought to have evolved from the British mob football (or Soule as the French called it), where a game would take place between two villages. The ball would be dropped in one village, and the two villages would try to keep the ball away from each other. This would often lead to scuffles and fights that could last for days. Eventually, in the early 19th century, universities in England wished to have universal rules set up for the sport, which saw the game being confined to a field with two goals and only 11 players over 90 minutes.

Since then, the game grew rapidly. The British exported the formalized game to every corner of the earth. Leagues and cups were established in many countries by the end of the 19th century. FIFA, the game's governing body, was set up in the early 20th century. The first World Cup took place in Uruguay in 1930, setting the stage for many moments of heroism and some of the game's greatest scenes over the next nearly one hundred years.

Introduction

Since those earliest days, as long as there have been football games and tournaments, there have been inspiring players. Stretching all the way back to the earliest F.A. Cups in England, the various leagues around the world, the Olympic Games, the World Cup tournaments which started in 1930, and the continental club competitions, the joy that these teams and their players have brought to the lives of so many people through the years is immeasurable. The players that brought about these magical moments have gone on to inspire many future legends. Some of these players are also ones we'll be taking a look at in this book.

Chapter 1:
Pele (1940 - 2022)

Pele (1940 - 2022)

> "Success is no accident. It is hard work, perseverance, learning, studying, sacrifice and most of all, love of what you are doing or learning to do." —
> Pele

Country: Brazil

Major Teams: Santos; New York Cosmos

Career Span: 1956 - 1977

Career Highlights: 6 Campeonato Brasileiro Serie A titles; 1 North American Soccer League Soccer Bowl; 3 FIFA World Cup titles; 7 Ballon d'Or awards; Time 100 Most Important People of the 20th Century; Reuters News Agency and International Olympic Committee's Athlete of the Century (1900-99); FIFA Player of the Century; Guinness World Records for most career goals (1363).

Humble Beginnings

Boxing had Muhammed Ali. Baseball had Babe Ruth. Ice Hockey had Wayne Gretzky. Basketball had Michael Jordan. Even if you ask someone who knows absolutely nothing about one of these sports which the greatest of all time is, chances are they'd still be likely to tell you these names. For soccer, there is only one name, Pele.

The player who the world would come to know as Pele was born Edson Arantes do Nascimento in 1941 in a very poor area of Brazil. He was named after American inventor Thomas Edison, as his parents had great hopes for their son. His father was a soccer player himself, who played for a number of clubs in Brazil. At the time, soccer players didn't earn that much money. The family couldn't even afford to buy the young and already soccer-mad Edson a soccer ball. One day, Edson and his friends decided to take one of his socks and stuffed it with paper to make his own ball. He would kick and play with this ball for hours against the wall and through the dusty street with other neighborhood kids. He would also sometimes literally choose soccer over food, when he would use fruit given to him (like mangoes) as a soccer ball.

Having a soccer player in the house certainly helped. Edson's father taught him the importance of fitness, and the art of dribbling, while the local kids also played their part in molding his flair and skills.

Pele (1940 - 2022)

What's in a Name?

Throughout his childhood years, Edson went by the nickname Dico, which was given to him by his family. He loved this nickname, as it meant Son of a warrior. For the boy who adored his father, you can only imagine why he loved this name so much.

At school, though, it was a different story. Edson had a bad way of pronouncing one of his favorite players' names. Instead of Bile, he would say Pile (which sounded more like Pele). To tease him, his classmates started calling him Pele. This name annoyed the young and usually happy-go-lucky boy so much that he would often shout at his classmates. One day, he hit a boy who called him Pele and was handed a two-day suspension (Hendrix, 2017b).

When he arrived home from school, we could only imagine the talking to he must have received from his parents. His parents would have understandably taught him an important lesson that day: A rose by any other name would smell just as sweet. Whether his classmates called him Edson, Dico, or Pele, it would make him a better or worse person. It also certainly would not make him a better or worse soccer player.

A few days later, the boy who used to be known as Dico returned to school. He tried his best to remember the lesson his parents had taught him, and from that day forward, he never again got angry when someone called him Pele. In fact, he learned to embrace the name. Whenever he scored a goal in one of the tournaments he played in, the crowd cheered, "Pele, Pele, Pele!" How could someone remain angry then?

Jinga What?

Pele's father would continue to play an instrumental role in his son's development. He would teach him all the tricks and skills he had learned and picked up over the years. The outlandish style of play, known as Jinga, was popular among the formerly enslaved, poorer population in Brazil. It was also the exact opposite of the structured way in which the European teams of the day played. While fun to watch, it didn't manage to help Brazil win any World Cup titles. And many critics blamed their style of play for this.

With every passing World Cup, the young Pele would remember watching his father cry every time Brazil was knocked out of the World Cup. For Pele, it was tough seeing the warrior in his life cry. He vowed that one day, he would bring the World Cup home to Brazil!

Pele (1940 - 2022)

Pele would eventually be spotted by soccer scouts and offered a place in the local junior team. It was not long before the teenage prodigy was promoted to the senior team and would play all across Brazil. Still only aged 17, it was considered a major shock when Pele was selected for the 1958 World Cup Brazilian team. The family celebrated all through the next few days, as did the village. It was considered such a momentous occasion that the young boy, who only a few years earlier was still shining shoes and playing soccer with the locals, would now be playing for Brazil.

Before he left, his father told him to believe in himself and not to let anyone else tell him how to play. Pele was understandably scared. He had never even met most of the adult men he would be playing with, but he found his teammates to all be very friendly, as they welcomed him with open arms. They realized they would need to stand together as a team if they wanted to finally bring the World Cup to Brazil.

When the team arrived in Sweden they were met with constant ridicule by the international press. "Brazil is a great team, but they should focus on winning matches rather than showing off their skills," was the common thought. Even the national team coach would tell Pele to not play that style of soccer, he didn't want himself embarrassed.

The team got off to a great start, as they easily made their way through to the quarterfinal. There was only one problem. Pele had not been given any game time yet. As the youngest player on the team, he was very shy and didn't want to ask his coach why he was asked to fly halfway across the world only to sit on the bench. Every match after the team was named and Pele wasn't in it, the coach would tell him he would get to play when the time was right. Almost as if he viewed Pele as the secret weapon that would unleash on an unsuspecting target.

In the quarterfinal against Wales, due to many injuries, Pele finally got his opportunity. The scores were level going into halftime, and the Brazilians were dejected. They were fed up with playing the European style of soccer, and the young Pele was encouraged by one of his senior teammates to play his own, more natural style of Jinga soccer. It would be a turning point for not only the young Pele but also for Brazilian soccer, which would never be the same again. Nor would the soccer world, for that matter! A different team came out in the second half, and Pele scored the game's only goal. In doing so, he became the youngest-ever player to score a goal at the World Cup. This win set up a date with France in the semifinal.

The team ran out onto the field with a renewed spirit. None more so than Pele. He attacked the ball, dribbled, and danced through

Pele (1940 - 2022)

the French defense. It was perhaps the finest showing of Jinga soccer ever, with the teenage Pele scoring a hat-trick in the second half! Brazil won the match 5-2 and booked their place in the World Cup final. The world was forced to sit up and take notice of the 17-year-old boy's wonder.

The team then prepared for the big final. Pele could not help but remember the country's only other World Cup final appearance when Brazil lost to Uruguay in 1950. The day he saw his warrior father crying. He was determined not to let this happen again. The team was now encouraged by their coach to embrace their natural style of play and selected a very attacking formation never seen before.

The final against Sweden was a highly entertaining affair. The soccer critics and experts were still of the opinion that there was no way Brazil could win. Surely, their Jinga style would once again fail them, they assumed. This time, though, the Brazilian machine was unstoppable. The Swedes drew first blood and scored first within four minutes of kick-off. They also targeted Pele and made sure not to give him too much room. They also laid in their tackles on the teenager. Brazil managed to fire back and equalize. After that it seemed like the Brazilians were dancing circles around the Swedish team, who were made to look like schoolboys.

"Shot, he scores!" "Pele shoots, Goal!" "Another goal for the Brazilians!" "What a shot! Another goal for the Brazilians. Five-one!" The game would eventually finish five-two to the Brazilians, and Pele and the team had done it. They had finally brought the World Cup home to Brazil. To the team, there was only one hero, the 17-year-old Pele. He was hoisted onto his teammate's shoulders and carried around the stadiums. At home, there were similar scenes of jubilation, with Pele's father again left in tears. This time, however, they were tears of joy. He couldn't believe that his dream had finally come true. And it was all thanks to his son, the youngest-ever winner of the World Cup.

Coming to America

After his first World Cup win with Brazil, Pele's career only went from strength to strength. By the time the next World Cup came in 1962, most considered him to be the best player in the world. He scored in Brazil's opening match but would, unfortunately, pick up an injury in the second match of the tournament. Brazil would go on to win the tournament, and Pele was now considered a two-time World Cup winner.

He would also go on to help Santos win 6 titles through the 1960s, scoring a high number of goals throughout the decade.

Pele (1940 - 2022)

Brazil wasn't able to win a hat-trick of titles in 1966 but returned stronger than ever in 1970. Pele played a pivotal role in helping Brazil win their third World Cup in front of a crowd of over 107,000, beating Italy 4-1 in the final (with Pele contributing the opening goal, of course). By becoming the first country to win the World Cup three times, they were allowed to keep the original Jules Rimet Trophy. The Brazilian team that won the World Cup that year has often been voted as the greatest team of all time (Collett, 2007).

In 1974, after 19 years at Santos, Pele decided it was time to retire, having already stopped playing for Brazil three years earlier. Between 1971 and 1974, Pele was unsure whether he should retire or move to a new club in Europe, like Real Madrid or Juventus, as so many had done before him. Clive Toye, the head of the New York Cosmos, had wanted for a long time to restore U.S. soccer to its glory since the early 1900s, culminating in their third-place finish at the first World Cup in 1930.

Toye hatched a plan that would see the U.S. become one of soccer's top destinations. For this plan to succeed though, he had to get Pele, who he considered the greatest player of all time, on board. In 1971, he traveled all the way to Jamaica, found out which hotel Santos was staying in, and snuck in. He found Pele lounging at the pool.

Toye started, "Hi. You don't know me, but I have a feeling we're going to get to know each other very well. My name is Clive Toye, and I want to make you even more popular than you already are. I am the general manager of the New York Cosmos, and I know that you're coming to the end of your career. You could go to Juventus, you could go to Real Madrid, yeah, you could win a championship. But so will other people. You come to us, you can win a country, and nobody else could do that except you."

The idea of "winning a country" appealed to Pele, and over the next few years, the pair would meet dozens more times. After Pele retired from Santos, and subsequently got bored of doing nothing, he decided to sign with the New York Cosmos. Pele was already in his mid-30s, but he was still on fire whenever he took the field. Pele's biggest contribution, however, was not on the field.

Soccer was not a very popular sport at the time. Behind American football, baseball, and ice hockey, the sport was probably at its lowest point in the 1970s. The Cosmos, for example, averaged around 3,500 fans at matches throughout the season before Pele arrived. In his first season at the club, the average crowd nearly tripled. A season later, it was at nearly 20,000. For Pele's final season at the club, there was an average crowd of 34,142 (Blum, 2022). By the time of his final ever

Pele (1940 - 2022)

professional match with the Cosmos, this who's who of the day was spotted in the crowd of around 75,500—Muhammad Ali, Mick Jagger, Henry Kissinger, Barbra Streisand, and Robert Redford were all there (McIntyre, 2022). It's absolutely incredible, considering that a few years earlier, the crowds were about the size of a popular school game. After his final game, which involved winning the Soccer Bowl, Pele was lifted up on his teammates' shoulders as the crowd chanted, "Pele! Pele! Pele!"

The effects were felt beyond just the crowds, though. Some of the world's other top soccer stars of the day suddenly saw the U.S. as a viable option. Franz Beckenbauer, Carlos Alberta, Giorgio Chinaglia, Johan Cruyff, Bobby Moore, George Best and Gordon Banks all came across the pond. The other league matches also saw a massive boost in attendance. TV ratings spiked, and the enrolment in soccer at schools and clubs suddenly exploded. The U.S. was seeing its greatest boom. Not bad for a sport that had been considered long dead. In 1988, the U.S. was chosen to host the 1994 World Cup. Many consider this to be the hosting of the World Cup, which was the culmination of the soccer boom that started with Pele's arrival.

There would be one last farewell match for Pele in October 1977. The previous five World Cup winning captains were present, as was President Carter's son to present Pele with a plaque before the match. It read:

"Presented to Pelé for the smiles he put on children's faces, the thrills he gave to fans of this nation and the dimension he added to American sports. Pelé has elevated the game of soccer to heights never before attained in America, and only Pelé, with his status, incomparable talent and beloved compassion, could have accomplished such a mission. The United States of America is deeply grateful."

Pele addressed the crowd with tears streaming down his face:

"Ladies and gentlemen, I am very happy to be there with you in this greatest moment of my life," he said. "I want to thank you all, every single one of you. I want to take this opportunity to ask you to pay attention to the young of the world, the children, the kids. We need them too much. Love is more important than what we can take in life," he said. "Everything passes. Please say with me three times – Love! Love! Love!" (Lewis, 2017)

Pele continued to serve not only the game of soccer but also various charities, causes, and even the Brazilian government over the next 40 years. He passed away in 2022, having lived a full and happy life. His place was secured as the greatest player to ever step onto the soccer field!

Pele (1940 – 2022)

Activities

1. Pele is generally considered to be the greatest soccer player of all time. Who is your favorite soccer player and why?

2. Pele did not initially like his nickname (Pele) and wanted to be called Dico. Have you or someone you know ever been called a name you did not like? How did you (or the other person) get people to stop using this name? Or did it simply become your (or their) normal nickname, like Pele?

3. Pele was told at his first World Cup to stop playing the Jinga style. He and his team eventually convinced the coach to let them play this style of soccer. Have you ever had to convince someone to let you do something that they told you not to? What was the situation, and was the end result better because your solution was used? How did you go about it?

Chapter 2:
President George Weah
(1966 -)

President George Weah (1966 -)

Education is a continual process, it's like a bicycle... If you don't pedal, you don't go forward. —George Weah

Country: Liberia

Major Teams: Mighty Barrolle; Invincible Eleven; Tonnerre Yaounde; Monaco; Paris Saint-Germain; AC Milan; Chelsea; Manchester City; Marseille; Al Jazira

Career Span: 1981 - 2003

Career Highlights: 2 Liberian Premier League titles; 1 Liberian FA Cup title; 1 Ligue 1 title; 3 Coupe de France titles; 2 Serie A titles; 1 FA Cup; 2 African Footballer of the Year awards; 1 Ballon d'Or award

Make Way For Weah

George Weah was born into some of the worst conditions one could ever imagine. He grew up in a poor neighborhood near Monrovia, Liberia, consisting mostly of mud brick structures (Tarpeh, n.d.). His family, like most, struggled to provide even the most basic necessities for themselves. Food on the table every night and a clean pair of clothing every morning were not guaranteed. His father also left the family when George was only three years old, and their mother, unable to care for him and his siblings, left them in the care of her mother, George's grandmother.

George enjoyed playing soccer with his friend. They didn't really have a field to play on or even a ball to play with, but they made do with what little they had, which usually included a ball being made out of rags. George's talents were spotted early on when he was invited to play with the local club. Despite only being 15 years old, he was instrumental in helping the team win two consecutive promotions.

The Wenger Bus is Coming

He would eventually be signed to play for a club in Cameroon. While playing for Tonnerre Yaoundé, the Cameroon national coach called an old friend, Arsene Wenger, who was managing Monaco at the time, and told him he believed he may have just found a rare diamond in the rough. Wenger flew out from Monaco to watch Weah play. He could not simply go on hearsay and sign a player because his friend said he should.

Wenger could not believe his eyes. He was astonished by how well the young Weah was playing. Passing defenders with ease,

President George Weah (1966 -)

creating opportunities, and taking those opportunities presented to him. One can just see the broad smile on the usually emotionless Wenger's face while sitting in the stands, believing he had just found what he believed to be Africa's greatest export.

He made Weah an offer to join Monaco, a French club. The young George was scared. The children of his country were always taught that the Europeans (especially white Europeans) were not to be trusted. For centuries, they had treated black Africans poorly, and this left a deep and multi-generational mistrust. None more so than Liberia, which was founded as a celebration of black liberty from oppression. Weah, however, went with his instinct. He placed his trust in Wenger, who he saw as someone speaking to him as a father to a son and giving him all the opportunities he would never receive if he decided to stay in Africa.

Weah was also worried as he didn't speak any French. It turned out there were a few teammates who spoke English, so that wasn't an issue. Wenger was also aware that the young Weah was stepping into unknown territory and would invite him to spend time with him and his family. George had finally found a father figure he could look up to. He describes Wenger as not only having the greatest impact on him as a player but also responsible for molding him into the man he would later become

(Winter, 2000).

Arsene looked after Weah, and Weah repaid him by always giving his best on the field in every match. It proved to be a match made in heaven. Weah couldn't stop scoring goals and was voted African Player of the Year in 1989.

Although he later moved to other clubs in France (Paris Saint Germain) and Italy (AC Milan), he would never forget the kindness shown by Wenger. When he became the first African player to win the FIFA World Player of the Year and the most prestigious award in football, the Ballon d'Or, in 1995, he made sure the world knew who deserved all the praise. He called Wenger up on stage, thanked him, and handed him the trophy. He wanted to make sure people across the world could see that it was possible for people from different race groups, different cultures, and different age groups to become the best of friends. Just as he and Wenger had.

Not Too Cool For School

At the time George Weah was growing up, schooling was not easily accessible. Formal education, in the way most first-world children know, never really existed for the poor. If you were

President George Weah (1966 -)

lucky enough, you would learn basic math and how to read before starting to work by the time you were a teenager. Try as he may, George only made it to high school and didn't graduate. He had, however, realized the importance of education and promised himself that one day he would finish school, even if he had to wait until he was an old man!

By the time George had retired from soccer, he was already viewed as not only Africa's greatest-ever soccer player but also a naturally born leader among men. Many encouraged him to get into politics, as Africa, and more specifically Liberia had been plagued by poor leadership and ravaged by civil war throughout his playing career.

In 2005, despite a lot of ridicule, the soccer player decided to run for president. He performed better than most expected, but critics, however, continued to focus on the fact that he had no formal education. George never forgot the promise he had made to himself, and he took this criticism as a sign that now was the time to finish his schooling. While many adults would be embarrassed, George set out to prove to the children and adults of his home nation that one should never be embarrassed to try something new, especially if it meant self-improvement.

Weah would eventually go on to obtain his high school diploma at the age of 41 and then continue studying Business Administration at DeVry University in Miami (Paye-Layleh, 2010). He had throughout his soccer career been involved in a lot of humanitarian work, especially encouraging children to attend schools and making sure schooling environments were in a better state than when he was younger. Occasionally, the children he spoke to would ask him about his own education. Now, with pride, he would be able to tell them that he had completed high school.

President Weah — African Pride

George Weah was by far the most popular person to have ever come from Liberia. This was before he ever entered the political arena. Many had begged him to stand for president, believing he could transform the country, just as he had at Monaco, PSG, and AC Milan. In 2014, he won a seat in the country's senate and looked poised for greater success.

Weah studied the great leaders of Africa intently, growing especially close to the great Nelson Mandela during his time as a UNICEF ambassador. It was Mandela who gave Weah the nickname "African Pride," believing there was no one who made Africans more proud (UNICEF, n.d.). A bold endorsement from a

President George Weah (1966 -)

man many consider to be among the greatest people to have ever lived.

In 2017, Liberia again held national elections. Many waited to see if Weah could finally fulfill his destiny. He won over 60% of the vote in the final round of voting and was sworn in as President of Liberia in January 2018. It was an important moment for the country, as it was the first time in 74 years that the country's power was handed over peacefully via a vote. Previous instances of political change were usually due to violent coups.

His term would come to an end in 2023, but not before he went on to accomplish one final feat that we'll probably never see again. He would play one final match for Liberia at age 51. In a friendly match against Nigeria, organized so that his number 14 jersey could be retired in a post-match ceremony, George Weah would become the first (and probably last) serving head of state to play in an international soccer match.

His good work and kind deeds he worked on during his time as a soccer player, a humanitarian and as president has and will continue to give millions hope and a chance at a life better than the world he was born into. George Weah's name will forever be etched in the book of not only the greatest soccer players of all time, but also of the greatest and most inspiring humans as well.

Activities

1. George Weah was raised by his grandmother, who taught him many important lessons he has carried with him throughout his life. What are some important lessons your grandparents (or aunts and uncles or older adults) have taught you?

2. George Weah had a great mentor in Arsene Wenger. Do you have any coaching mentors in soccer or other sports? What are some things they have taught you or acts of kindness they have shown you?

3. George Weah believed that education was important and even went back to finish his schooling much later in life than most people. Ask your parent (or an older adult) what are some things they accomplished a lot later in life than most other people have.

Chapter 3:
Mia Hamm (1972 -)

"I learned a long time ago that there is something worse than missing the goal, and that's not pulling the trigger." —Mia Hamm

Country: United States of America

Major Teams: North Carolina Tar Heels; Washington Freedom

Career Span: 1986 - 2004

Career Highlights: 4 NCAA National Championship titles; 2 FIFA World Cup titles (1991, 1999); 2 Olympic Gold medals (1996, 2004); 1 WUSA Founders Cup titles; 1 Major Soccer League Cup (as part owner)

Overcoming

Mia Hamm was born in 1972 to a family who moved frequently due to her father being a pilot in the U.S. Air Force. She was the fourth of six children and had her back against the wall from a young age. She was born with a defect, partial clubfoot (her feet were twisted out of a normal position). To correct the issue, casts were placed on her feet. When they came off, doctors were confident that the issue had been fixed. Her family always joked that the morning before the casts came off was the last time they saw her not running (CNN, 2001).

The family found themselves in Italy when little Mia was a

Mia Hamm (1972 -)

toddler. It was here where she first discovered what the locals called *Calcio*. Her family recalls how she took a soccer ball from an older kid at a local park. Try as the kid may, he couldn't retrieve the ball from between Mia's feet. If ever there was a sign of things to come, this was certainly it.

The Hamms embraced their daughter's love of the sport at a very early age. By the time Mia was five years old, the family moved back to the U.S. They had also adopted a Thai-American orphan named Garrett. Although he was three years older than Mia, the two were inseparable. The Hamm parents decided to sign both Mia and Garrett up for the local soccer team.

Once Mia started school, she wanted nothing more than to play soccer every day. Her school, unfortunately, had no girls' team. Mia didn't care and showed her uncompromising way early on. She had trained with Garrett and his friends her whole life, which only toughened her up. Garrett even insisted that his friends not make things easy on her just because she was a girl, even though she was much younger than them. So why couldn't she play against the boys her own age?

Luckily, the school allowed her to play. She was supported by everyone, including her boy teammates. She played so well that she became something of a local sensation. Due to a lack of girls' clubs and opportunities to play, she was forced to join a North Texas regional team despite only being 14. This is where her celebrity status grew, with her coaches speaking highly of her speed, athleticism, and natural instincts.

Then the unthinkable happened. Mia, still aged just 15, was chosen to represent the U.S. in the U.S. Olympic Festival. In doing so, she became the youngest-ever player to represent her country. An incredible achievement for the young, blossoming talent. Observers were stunned at how mature this little girl was playing. The legend of Mia Hamm was born.

Triumphs to Tragedy to Triumph

FIFA finally decided that 1991 was the right time to host the first Women's World Cup (61 years after the first men's World Cup). Hamm was an integral part of the U.S. Team by this point and was a shoo-in as a member of the squad.

The U.S. team was dominant throughout the tournament and would go undefeated on route to the final, even beating the heavily fancied Germany 5-2 in the semifinals. The U.S. would go on to be crowned champions after beating Norway 2-1 in the final. It was the first time ever that a U.S. team had won an

Mia Hamm (1972 -)

international soccer tournament. Hamm was still barely in her twenties but was already considered by most to be one of the best players in the world.

By the time the 1996 Atlanta Olympics rolled around, there was extra pressure on the Women's team to win in front of their home crowd. For Hamm, there was a much more personal battle closer to home. Her older brother Garrett, who had been instrumental in her development as a soccer player during her formative years, was diagnosed with a rare blood disorder called aplastic anemia. Garrett and the family was told shortly before the Olympics that he didn't have long to live. Even in his weakened state, he promised Mia he would be there to watch the final if the U.S. made it.

Hamm just knew that winning the gold medal was the only option. She knew that doing so wouldn't cure her beloved brother of his disease, but it would at least make him extremely happy during the days filled mostly with pain. Hamm and the U.S. team would become the darlings of the Atlanta games.

The U.S. started off well. However, in a cruel twist of fate, Hamm picked up injuries to her foot and ankle in the second match. Journalists at the time compared it to Michael Jordan, widely considered to be the greatest basketball player at the time, hobbling off the court (Dufresne, 1996), leaving her future in the tournament up in the air. One could only imagine how much inspiration she drew from Garrett, who was going through a far greater fight. She reminded herself constantly why she had to do all she could to make it to the finals!

With the massive crowds fully behind them, the U.S. team plowed their way through the competition and progressed to the finals against China. There was another swerve in Hamm's story, though, as she picked up an injury to her groin (and was still suffering from a sore ankle).

As the teams took the field for the final in front of over 76,000 fans, Hamm scanned the stadium to find Garrett. She must have been thinking about all the lessons he taught her and all their memories created on the soccer field and off the field. How Garret had taught her to always go on hard to win the ball from the older boys she played against. How she should always keep the ball close to her feet at all times. How he taught her to always remain humble, and how he always encouraged her to seize every opportunity. This was her opportunity to say thank you.

Hamm had a great match and was instrumental in setting up the first goal scored by the U.S. The Chinese team would go on to draw level later in the first half. Hamm and her teammates came

Mia Hamm (1972 -)

out of the changing rooms fired up after the halftime break. With 22 minutes to go, the golden girl of U.S. soccer once again stepped up and played a pivotal role in setting up what would become the winning goal!

The U.S. supporters held their breath when Hamm went down with another injury a minute before full-time. Luckily, the U.S. team was able to hang on. When all was said and done, the U.S. team beat China 2-1. The team had done it; they had won the gold medal in front of a rapturous crowd (Gildea, 1996)! For Hamm, the victory meant so much more. She knew that winning the gold medal would mean the world to her family, especially Garrett. It provided a brief glimmer of joy in what would be their most difficult time. The family celebrated together that week for the final time.

Garrett would pass away less than a year later. While devastated at losing her brother, best friend, and idol, she understood that with her newfound fame, she could turn this negative experience into a positive. She would go on to find the Mia Hamm Foundation. The non-profit organization raises awareness and funds for families with loved ones fighting bone marrow and core blood issues. The foundation has raised millions of dollars for this cause and continues to make a difference in the lives of many.

If It Doesn't Exist, Create It

The U.S. Women's team has enjoyed great success over the years. Rising up from relative obscurity in the 1980s when Hamm was first selected to represent her country, to the great success they experienced at the 1991 World Cup and the 1996 Olympic Games. The Olympic Gold Medal victory especially did a lot to raise awareness of the women's game.

Owing to the success of the 1996 Olympics, the U.S. was selected to host the 1999 Women's World Cup. Tens of thousands packed the stadiums for the matches as the U.S. ladies ran rampant. They steamrolled their way into the finals, where they once again beat China to claim their second World Cup title.

Mia Hamm was among the players who couldn't help but wonder how it was that there was still no professional women's league anywhere in the world. The earliest men's leagues were already over 100 years old. In the top leagues in other countries, even the lesser-known players of the top teams earned millions. Yet, many of the women soccer players representing their countries were still working other day jobs to make ends meet. The World Cup proved once and for all that the women could pack stadiums and draw TV ratings just like the men could. "Maybe it was time to start the first women's league," was the common thought by

Mia Hamm (1972 -)

many of the top female players of the day.

Luckily, there were many who felt the same way, including financial backers and TV networks. With Hamm as one of the key names behind the scenes and in front of the cameras, the Women's United Soccer Association was founded in February 2000. It was the first women's league in the world, and the face of the league was none other than Mia Hamm (McDonogh, 2011).

The league would only last three seasons before most financial backers withdrew investments. The WUSA laid the foundation for other leagues, including the National Women's Soccer League, which was founded in 2012 and continues to this day with Hamm as a partial owner of two teams. Many believe that none of these leagues would ever have been possible without Hamm's involvement and initial push for it in the late 1990s.

For the role she played in developing the game of soccer both on and off the field, there is simply no greater legend than Mia Hamm. The women's game would simply not be on the international level of popularity had she never played. Her record number of goals and appearances, the number of trophies she was involved in bringing home, and lastly, in retirement, for her continued fight to bring the women's game into the same limelight as the men's, the name of Mia Hamm will live on forever in the game of soccer.

Activities

1. Mia Hamm moved around a lot as a child. Have you or any of your friends had to move from one town or city to another? What challenges did you or they face when arriving in the new town or city?

2. Mia Hamm was especially close to her older brother Garrett. Do you have an older sibling, cousin, or friend who you are close to? What are some things they have taught you about life?

3. Women's soccer, for a long time, did not have a league like the men did, and Mia Hamm was involved in starting the first Women's League in the U.S. Describe one situation in which there was something you really wanted but it didn't exist, and you were forced to make it.

Chapter 4:
David Beckham OBE (1975-)

"I always say that practice gets you to the top most of the time." —David Beckham

Country: England

Major Teams: Manchester United; Preston North End; Real Madrid; LA Galaxy; AC Milan; Paris Saint-Germain

Career Span: 1992 - 2013

Career Highlights: 6 Premier League titles; 2 FA Cup titles; 1 UEFA Champions League; 1 La Liga title; 2 Major Soccer League Cup titles; 1 Ligue 1 title; BBC Sport Personality of the Year Lifetime Achievement Award; English Football Hall of Fame; Premier League Hall of Fame

Learning to Bend It Like Beckham

David Beckham grew up in South London to working-class parents. From an early age, young David was already crazy about soccer. He could not wait for the school day to end every day, as this meant he and his friends could go play soccer. He realized early on that he was not as fast as some of the other kids, and he also didn't quite have their flashy skills. He had, however, noticed that he was a lot more accurate with his passes and

David Beckham OBE (1975 -)

shots. David wished to become a master of set pieces. Free kicks and corners would become his specialty.

When he was a little older and started playing for the local club's youth team, David would wait impatiently for his father to arrive home from work. As soon as his father arrived home, the two would make their way over to the local club's field. David's father would help his son practice his free kicks. David would place the ball, and his father would stand in such a position that would force David to curve the ball around him. The father and son would often have the locals startled, as they would practice for hours every day and into the evening until it was dark.

The pair would then walk back home, but David's soccer fix would still sometimes not be satisfied. There was a strict family rule in the Beckham household: No soccer balls in the house! This meant David had to find an alternative. He would make use of his sister's teddy bears and further practice his free kick accuracy, often angering his mother and sister.

All this hard work would pay off, though. By the time he was a teenager, he had been snapped up by Tottenham Hotspur's Youth team. He had already gained a reputation for having a deadly right boot on freekicks and corners. So much so, that opposition teams were scared to give free kicks away anywhere close to the goals, as they knew Beckham would find a way to bend it through their defence and test their goalkeeper's abilities. A true testament to how hours of hard work and practice pay off in the end.

World Cup Zero to National Hero

David Beckham joined Sir Alex Ferguson's Manchester United in the early 1990s and linked up with other future legends like Ryan Giggs, Paul Scholes, the Neville Brothers, and Nicky Butt. These players were all still considered developmental talents at the time. These players would go on to form the core of the team that would win title after title over the next decade. David Beckham, for his part, had become one of the most feared set-piece takers in the entire world by the late 1990s. The opposition also learned not to give him too much room to shoot from far out after a particularly famous goal from inside his own half.

He was an England regular by the time the 1998 World Cup rolled around, and the English supporters once again had it in their mind that this England side would be the one to finally emulate their 1966 heroes and go all the way. Beckham had recently started dating his future wife, Victoria, a member of the world's hottest girl band at the time, the Spice Girls. Many vocal critics

David Beckham OBE (1975 -)

thought Beckham should focus on his soccer and less on the glitz and glamor lifestyle they thought he was getting caught in.

In the 1998 World Cup, England progressed to the round of 16 knockout stages and came up against their old foes, Argentina. It was a match for the ages and one that not many would soon forget. For Beckham, though, it would be for the wrong reasons. After going down by one goal after five minutes, England clawed their way back to take the lead by the 16th minute. Just before half time, Argentine drew level. The teams were level at halftime, with the England players visibly disappointed that they allowed the Argentines back into the match.

The fired-up England team took to the field for the second half. Within the first minute, there was an incident. Diego Simeone had fouled Beckham. He went in so hard from behind that he knocked both himself and Beckham down. Beckham fell face-first into the field, and Simeone took the opportunity to cheekily push Beckham's face further into the ground. This would no doubt have seen Simeone receive a few years later, but it was considered part of the game at that point. With a rush of blood to the head, Beckham kicked out at Simeone and tripped him as he was getting up. As is often the case in soccer, the player retaliating received a harsher punishment. The commentators could not believe it, "David Beckham. Red card!"

As it was a World Cup knockout match, the match would go to penalties if the scores remained level after full time plus the extra 30 minutes of play. Beckham would have been expected to take a penalty had he still been on the field. Instead, the brave 10-man England managed to hang on for 90 minutes plus the 30 minutes of extra time to force the match into a penalty shootout. England would go on to lose that match, and just about every Tom, Dick, and Harry laid the blame squarely at the door of one person, David Beckham!

The press crucified him, as did some of his teammates. He even received death threats, and his posters and effigies of him were being burned in the streets. It was only after a phone call from Ferguson the morning after the match that Beckham was ready to face the world again. Sure, he felt like he had let his team and country down, but did a 23-year-old really deserve this backlash? Over the coming months, he would be heavily booed whenever he touched the ball; it seemed like the entire England had turned on him. One could easily have imagined a player with less thick skin packing it in and leaving England altogether.

Beckham decided to stick it out, though. He had a great support base of management and friends. Moreover, if there was one thing he loved, it was proving the critics wrong.

David Beckham OBE (1975 -)

Beckham set out to rewrite his story. He was a part of the historic Manchester United team that won the treble in 1999 (winning the English Premier League, the F.A. Cup, and the UEFA Champion's League) and would go on to captain England from the turn of the century. Attempting to qualify for the 2002 World Cup, England was on the verge of being knocked out, as they were trailing Greece 2-1 after 90 minutes of play. Needing a draw to secure qualification, England won a free kick outside the Greek box. There was never any doubt as to who would take the free kick, but could he convert it?

As he had done so many times as a youth when practicing with his dad, Beckham curled the ball into the top corner of the net as the stadium erupted! The commentator acknowledged that Beckham had pretty much led England to the World Cup single-handedly.

There was one final chapter to this story arc. At the 2002 World Cup, England and Argentina were drawn in the same group. Argentina won their opening match, while England managed to win only a draw. Many assumed the Argentine side would cruise through the group stages and thought England might struggle to make it out of the group of death.

Argentina then came up against England in the second match of the group stages. All eyes were on Beckham. Late in the first half, England was awarded a penalty. Many wondered if Beckham would step up to the plate, given the pressure that must have still been weighing heavily on his mind since that fateful day in 1998. Courageous as ever, he told his teammates to give him the ball. Even his former foe Simeone directed a chirp and a glance his way as he readied himself.

Beckham smashed the ball into the net and celebrated with delight. He repeatedly kissed his England jersey, happy to have finally proven those critics wrong. Never again was his love of his country questioned. His goal would be the only one of the match, and he ended up sending Argentina home early from the World Cup. This was the sweetest revenge. Although England would get knocked out by the tournament's eventual winner, Brazil, they were considered by many to be amongst the best teams at the World Cup. This was mainly down to their great captain.

Beckham still often describes that period after the 1998 World Cup as the toughest time of his life. Especially at the time, one can only imagine how tough it must have been. Perhaps we should remember for the future, the problems that seem like mountains today, will hopefully in three, five, or even ten years, only seem like molehills.

David Beckham OBE (1975 -)

To Real Galaxies... Far, Far Away

David Beckham's Manchester United had started to sense a turning of the tide by 2003. Many of the players that Beckham grew up with at the club had either been let go to make way for more international talent or had grown out of favor with the management and coaching staff. This, coupled with the fact that teams like Arsenal and Chelsea were starting to challenge Manchester United's dominance, led to increased frustrations for many of the players and management.

David Beckham was being targeted more and more as someone who was more concerned with his public image than his exploits on the field. He was, after all, probably the world's most recognizable soccer star. There had long been rumors that Real Madrid were gunning for Beckham's signature in the hopes of exploiting his fame with their great marketing machine.

After another Manchester United loss, their manager Ferguson flew into a fit of rage. He kicked a soccer boot, which hit Beckham. The stud split his eyebrow open, and in the heat of the moment, the two nearly got into a scuffle. It had become clear that Beckham's time at Manchester United was drawing to a close.

He wound up leaving at the end of the season and signing for Real Madrid in 2003. As predicted, the move launched Beckham into the celebrity stratosphere, which few soccer players had reached before. In Southeast Asia, they even compared the scenes upon his arrival for some friendly matches to that of the Beatles in the U.S. in the 1960s, aptly naming it Beckham-mania. Beckham, however, was determined to prove that he was more than just a marketing ploy used to line the pockets of the Real Madrid bosses.

He emphatically proved the critics wrong once again by fighting his way into the preferred starting line-up alongside what was considered to be one of the strongest soccer teams to ever take to a field. He more than held his own, being considered one of the top players in his time at the club, especially with his assists, and picking up a few trophies along the way.

In 2007, Beckham set out to see if he could provide the American market with the same boost it saw when Pele arrived. He signed for LA Galaxy, and there was an immediate air of excitement. Suddenly, stadiums were selling out, and TV ratings were through the roof. He was, unfortunately, not able to make much of a difference in his first few seasons at the club. He also played for Italian outfit AC Milan in the MLS offseason.

David Beckham OBE (1975 -)

His final few seasons at LA Galaxy proved to be much more fruitful, winning their conference twice and the MLS Cup twice. He then decided it was time to move back to Europe, where he ended his career playing for Paris Saint Germain, winning the league title.

David Beckham Superstar

Few soccer players have enjoyed the crossover success David Beckham has in the pop culture zeitgeist. Some ten years after his soccer career ended, many might not even be aware that he was once a soccer player.

He has gone on to launch successful business ventures that are not limited to fragrances, clothing, accessories, has acted in movies, and appeared on reality shows. He is also well known for being one of the most giving sports stars, and he can continuously be seen at charity events, lending his name and resources to worthy causes.

From his humble beginnings when he couldn't afford to join a club, to becoming probably the most well-known soccer player of his day, David Beckham certainly serves as a shining example as to what you can achieve if you put in the hard work.

Activities

1. David Beckham and his father would practice for hours on their local soccer field. Do you have any activities you and your father or older male relative enjoy doing together? What do you enjoy most about this activity?

2. David Beckham was treated rather unfairly after the 1998 World Cup but eventually answered his critics by helping England qualify for the next World Cup. Have you ever been treated unfairly for a mistake? How did you go about rectifying the situation

3. David Beckham was known as a great leader who stepped up when his country needed him most. Who is a leader, in or outside of soccer, you really admire? What qualities do you look for in a great leader?

Chapter 5:
Didier Drogba (1978 -)

"People have an opinion of Africa, and it is not so good, but we have to let sport unite us all." — Didier Drogba

Country: Ivory Coast

Major Teams: Le Mans; Guingamp; Marseille; Chelsea; Shangai Shenhua; Galatasary; Montreal Impact; Phoenix Rising

Career Span: 1998 - 2018

Career Highlights: 4 Premier League titles; 4 FA Cup titles; 1 UEFA Champions League title; 1 Super Lig title; 1 Turkish Cup; 2 African Footballer of the Year awards (2006, 2009); GQ Sportsman of the Year (2010); Time Top 100 (2010); Premier League Hall of Fame; Ivory Coast's all-time top goalscorer (65 goals)

Bon Jour, Didier

Didier Drogba's journey to become one of the most admired soccer players of all time was anything but conventional. He was born in Abidjan but moved to France at age five to live with his uncle. His uncle, Michel Goba, was a professional soccer player, and he convinced Didier's parents that there were many more

Didier Drogba (1978 –)

opportunities for the young boy in France. "Tito," as his parents nicknamed him, did not really want to leave his parents, but they tried to explain how moving to France would give him a real chance to succeed in life.

Tito traveled with his uncle for three seasons. His uncle also made sure that he always performed well in school. To ensure his marks were kept up to scratch, his uncle used to bribe him with shirts he exchanged with other players. After the end of the third season, it had become evident to Goba that Didier needed to return home. One can't begin to imagine how much the eight-year-old boy missed his parents after not seeing them for three years (Didier Drogba: My Childhood, n.d.).

He returned to Ivory Coast, and his family and friends were overjoyed. His friends had so many questions about France. "What were the people like?" "What food did you eat?" "What music do they listen to?" "Are their soccer players better than ours?" The young Didier enjoyed answering all these questions, but more than that, he loved being able to show off some of the new skills and tricks his uncle taught him. He and his friends were always organizing soccer matches in a local car park.

Three years after he returned to Ivory Coast, the country experienced economic collapse. His parents also fell victim to the conditions and lost their jobs. Didier's world was once again turned upside down when his parents again asked his uncle to take him in as they were struggling to provide even the basic needs to Didier. Goba agreed to take his nephew in again and with that, Didier had to pack his bags once again and leave his friends and family behind.

"Get Up Front"

Things were a little different this time around for Didier. Even at this young age, he was made aware that he would probably not be going back to the Ivory Coast, as his parents were planning to move to France.

Didier had always been an academically strong student, often finishing at the top of his class. He had also become even more obsessed with soccer. Instead of the car parks they used to play on in Ivory Coast, he and his friends would have proper fields to play on. They would play until it was time to go home for dinner. As a result of these long-playing hours, Didier's schoolwork began to suffer.

His grades got so bad that he was forced to repeat a grade. His parents had just arrived in France and decided to take action

Didier Drogba (1978 -)

fast! They sent him to live with a cousin in a different part of France where his naughty friends wouldn't be able to distract him. He was also banned from playing soccer for the next year, and they asked his teachers to keep an eye on him at all times. On the first day of the following school year, his teacher called, "Didier, get up front! I want to be able to see you!"

Over the following year, his grades improved, and he returned to live with his parents and siblings. His uncle also decided it was the right time to enroll him in a soccer club. He went to his first practice and was told he was going to play right back. He accepted his coach's decision. He was excited when he was first selected to play in his first organized soccer match and invited his uncle to come watch. His uncle was equally excited, as he had always hoped that the young boy he raised would follow in his footsteps.

Didier and his team took to the field, but the day didn't quite go as planned. From everything his uncle had seen since he first watched him play at age five, he believed Didier to be a natural-born goal scorer. We can only imagine the look of shock on his uncle's face when Didier lined up at right back for the team. "What is he doing," Goba must have wondered.

As many parents and supporters do at youth games, his uncle

was rather vocal on the sidelines that day. He repeatedly yelled at Didier, "Get up front!" The young Didier didn't want to disrespect his coach, but he agreed with his uncle. He wasn't a right-back, and his style of play was better suited to a forward. He pushed forward whenever he could and wowed the crowd with his skills.

After the match on their journey home, his uncle continued to question him, "What are you doing stuck back there? You need to get up front! In football, people only look at the strikers." Didier agreed he would have to talk with his coach about switching positions. However, when he arrived at the next practice before he could even discuss this with his coach, the coach called him aside and told him he would be playing up front from now on. He had obviously shown enough talent in the match the week before to convince his coach he had made a mistake. This would be the stepping stone he would need. Scoring goals at will, he slowly but surely began to make a name for himself, and as his uncle suggested, he would get noticed sooner rather than later.

Stop the Fighting

As Drogba's career was taking off in the early 2000s, there was

Didier Drogba (1978 -)

trouble back home. Civil war had broken out in his home nation of the Ivory Coast between the government-controlled South and the rebel-stronghold North. The fighting continued for two years but had thankfully ended by 2004. In 2005, though, it seemed like tensions were rising again and civil war would once again break out.

It was around this time that Drogba started making a name for himself as part of a star-studded Chelsea team. He was also part of possibly the strongest-ever Ivory Coast team. This team was on the verge of qualifying for their first World Cup. They successfully defeated Sudan in their last qualifier and needed Egypt to beat or draw with Cameroon in order to qualify. Drogba and his teammates huddled around a radio and waited for news from the Cameroon-Egypt match. Egypt had just drawn level but then conceded a penalty. The Ivory Coast players held their breaths and erupted when they heard that Cameroon had missed the penalty, which meant that Ivory Coast had qualified for the first-ever World Cup!

Even though Drogba was not one of the senior players, he was one of the most well-known. He proved that he would indeed make a fine leader when the media entered the Ivory Coast locker room to capture their live reactions to having qualified for the World Cup. With his teammates standing arm-in-arm around him, Drogba took a microphone and delivered a message to the troubled nation:

"Men and women of Ivory Coast. From the north, south, centre, and west, we proved today that all Ivorians can coexist and play together with a shared aim - to qualify for the World Cup. We promised you that the celebrations would unite the people - today, we beg you on our knees (the players all got down on their knees). The one country in Africa with so many riches must not descend into war. Please lay down your weapons and hold elections."

The players then sang, "We want to have fun, so stop firing your guns." As their celebrations continued, Drogba hoped and prayed that his words were heard by the government and rebels. There was no way they couldn't have, as the clip was played repeatedly across TV stations over the coming days and weeks.

In 2007, Drogba was touring through Ivory Coast as he had just won the African Footballer (Soccer Player) of the Year Award and wished to share his joy with his countrymen. Drogba was from the South, yet he did not exclude the northern region of Ivory Coast from his celebration. In fact, he announced that Ivory Coast would be playing their next match in the north—The rebel-held area that had previously been shunned by the

Didier Drogba (1978 –)

government when determining fixtures.

No one knows if Drogba was given permission to do this, but he saw the cause for peace in his homeland as a much greater one than even his own career. He knew there was every chance that the Ivory Coast government could have banned him for life, but it was a chance he was willing to take for national unity. Thankfully, they thought better than banning the African Footballer of the Year.

In the match itself, Ivory Coast would beat Madagascar 5-0, with Drogba scoring the final goal. Drogba, a southern-born player, took a lap of honor around the field in the north to rapturous applause and screams. For this brief moment in time, the Ivory Coast team had provided hope to the war-torn nation. They had stopped a civil war, and the key figure in the middle was Didier Drogba (Guilberteau, 2020)!

He went on to win many trophies and awards over his playing career, but his off-the-field humanitarian causes are undoubtedly what has set him apart from many others from his generation. He continues to this day to reach out and improve the lives of not only the Ivory Coast and African people but also those across the world. There are simply too many causes to list that he has been hands-on involved in, and it is impossible to have ever thought that he could ever have transcended his exploits on the field with this.

Activities

1. Didier Drogba's parents really valued a good education. What is your favorite subject in school? What do you enjoy about this subject?

2. As a youth, Didier Drogba traveled to France. What has been your favorite vacation destination? What did you enjoy most about this vacation?

3. Didier Drogba loves his country, Ivory Coast, dearly. What are some things you love most about your country?

Chapter 6:
Zlatan Ibrahimovic
(1981 –)

"When people criticize me, instead of putting my head down, it gives me energy to do even more." — Zlatan Ibrahimovic

Country: Sweden

Major Teams: Malmo FF; Ajax; Juventus; Inter Milan; Barcelona; AC Milan; Paris Saint-Germain; Manchester United; LA Galaxy

Career Span: 1998 - 2023

Career Highlights: 2 Eredivisie titles; 7 Serie A titles (2 later revoked); 1 La Liga title; 4 Ligue 1 titles; 1 FIFA Puskas Award; 2 UEFA Euro Goal of the Tournament awards (2004, 2012); GQ Men of the Year (2013); Sweden's all-time top goalscorer; Most MLS goals in a season (2019)

Bicycle, Kicks

Some soccer stars will tell you how soccer saved their lives, and there is perhaps no one to whom this saying is more true than Zlatan Ibrahimovic. He was born in Sweden, but his father was a Muslim Bosniak and his mother a Catholic Croat. Both had fled their individual war-torn countries, looking for a better life in Sweden. From a very early age, the young Zlatan had to learn to

Zlatan Ibrahimovic (1981 –)

be tough in order to survive (Kelly, 2013).

His parents fought constantly, often violently, and were divorced when Zlatan was still very young. He initially lived with his mother but remained in contact with his father. His mother physically abused him, and social services eventually placed him with his father. Life with his father was not much easier, as he was often saddened by the war situation back in his home country. He would then drink too much and had little money to care for Zlatan. Zlatan remembers how some of these tough times brought the two together, such as when his father bought him a bed but couldn't afford the delivery fee. Zlatan and his father carried the bed all the way from the shop back home (Hendrix, 2017a). He learned an important lesson that day. Even if two people don't always get along, they can still work together to accomplish a goal.

The rough life for Zlatan continued through his teenage years. He was very self-conscious about his lips, his big nose, and his mixed heritage. He felt like he didn't fit in anywhere, but eventually found a group of boys who also felt like outsiders in "normal" society. Unfortunately, these boys were petty thieves. They would steal sweets from shops, then food and drinks, and as they got older, they switched to stealing bicycles.

There was one saving grace for Zlatan though. At age six he had received his first pair of soccer boots. He enjoyed playing soccer through his teenage years with his friends when they weren't up to no good. Their field was a small, dusty piece of ground, and their objective was not so much to score goals as much as they looked to use tricks to get passed other players.

By age 14, he was part of the local Malmo FF's youth setup. He also started working on the docks to earn some extra money. He often butted heads with his coaches, his teammates, and their parents. He was actually on the verge of quitting the team, but his coach convinced him to stay. He explained how he thought Zlatan had a great future in the sport, and it could offer him a way out of his current, dead-end circumstances. Zlatan decided to play a few more years and was eventually selected for the Malmo senior side. It was only at this point that he realized that there was perhaps a better way of life waiting for him and his loved ones if he stuck to playing soccer. Soon, his undeniable talents were spotted by international eyes.

Zlatan Doesn't Do Auditions

By age 19, the awkward teen with the tough upbringing had grown into a towering young man. The 6'5" striker had also

Zlatan Ibrahimovic (1981 –)

become very confident in his own talents and knew his worth. One of the first clubs to scout his talents was Arsenal, whose manager, Arsene Wenger, had become well-known for spotting young talents over the years and getting the best out of them.

He and his team were very impressed with what they saw in Ibrahimovic. They had just finished 2nd in the league and were perhaps looking to build for the future by signing Ibrahimovic. Ibrahimovic would be joining a club that already boasted an impressive strike force of Dennis Bergkamp, Davor Suker, Nwankwo Kanu, and Thierry Henry.

He flew out to London to meet with Wenger and his team and claims that the welcome he received was a bit frosty. The final straw for Ibrahimovic was when, instead of offering him a contract, Wenger asked him to join the club on a trial. This was normal for younger and relatively unknown players, but Ibrahimovic was convinced he was a league above this. He told Wenger, "Zlatan doesn't do auditions," and thanked him for the offer (Eurosport, 2015). He was so assured of his talents that he turned down this opportunity most could only dream of.

It was a massive gamble, but one that would pay off. He was offered deals by a few big European clubs but eventually chose Ajax. The team seemed to be a good fit for him, even though it took him a season to find his feet. He scored goals at a phenomenal rate and helped the team to win two titles. His popularity was further boosted in 2004, when his goal against NAC Breda, which reminded many of the type of runs Diego Maradona became famous for, was voted goal of the year (Zlatan's Career, 2008). He was well and truly on his way, and the world was his oyster.

Brand Zlatan

Ibrahimovic has built quite a legacy since he left Sweden for the first time. He played for many European giants and either helped make them or cemented their position as some of the greatest teams of the time.

He also gained the reputation for being a player who was full of himself, although he, and most others that know him well will tell you it's all just confidence. Confidence, mind you, that is and has proven to be well-placed match after match and season after season. He also went on to build his name as brand by constantly referring to himself in the third person. "Zlatan had a great match," or "Zlatan is Sweden's greatest ever player," he'd often say.

Zlatan Ibrahimovic (1981 –)

He had a good reason for building his name as a brand, though. It got him noticed, after all, and would not only increase his value and self-worth but also would allow him to use his name for a greater good. While he might not have had the name recognition or received the accolades his counterparts Cristiano Ronaldo and Lionel Messi would, he was easily inside the top 10 most recognizable soccer players for the better part of the decade and a half before his retirement. His well-known name also allowed him to fulfill some personal promises he had made himself, to help those less fortunate than himself.

He has always supported many charitable organizations and worthy causes. One of these organizations in which Ibrahimovic has been very involved is the World Food Programme. It's a cause close to his heart, as he remembers his own family's struggle when he was young, how there was often nothing for him to eat at dinner time. He appeared in one of the most memorable advertisements ever produced featuring a soccer player.

"My name is Zlatan Ibrahimovic. Wherever I go, people recognize me. Call my name. Cheer for me. But there are names no one cheers for: Carmen, Rahma, Antoine, Lida, Chheuy, Mariko.

If I could, I would write every single name on my body. But there are 805 million names suffering from hunger in the world today. Too many of them are children. They are struck by war, natural disasters, and extreme poverty. I have supporters all over the world. Beginning today, I want the support to go to the people who really need it. So, whenever you hear my name, you will think of their names.

Whenever you see me, you will see them." (World Food Programme, 2015)

As he speaks the final words, Ibrahimovic removes his shirt and shows the names of these people mentioned tattooed across his body. A powerful image, one that many will have a hard time simply forgetting. It was moving and mesmerizing all at the same time, and most importantly, it got the message across.

He is also known for always going the extra mile when it comes to making children's wishes to meet him (and his teammates) come true. He does not mind making detours that many would consider too consuming, nor does he mind missing his bus or a flight if it involves spending more time with supporters, he feels need it. Of course, he can remember his days as a troubled youth and how much a day with one of his heroes would have meant. Maybe it would even have straightened him out earlier. At the

Zlatan Ibrahimovic (1981 –)

various clubs he's been at throughout his career, he is often the first to sign up to sign autographs, spend an afternoon training with the kids, or deliver Christmas presents.

While he may have been one of the best players of his generation, it is debatable whether he will be remembered for his spectacular goals, his "never say die" attitude, his extensive work with charities, or for being a so-called bad boy of soccer. Perhaps everyone should just take a page out of his books when he urges people to not judge a person if you don't know them.

Activities

1. Zlatan Ibrahimovic was known to have a short temper as a boy. What was something that used to anger you but no longer does? How did you learn to control your temper?

2. Zlatan Ibrahimovic's trial at Arsenal didn't lead to him getting signed with the club, but things worked out for the best in the end. What was something you thought you badly wanted at one stage, didn't get, and later felt it was for the better? How did things turn out better for you?

3. Zlatan Ibrahimovic does a lot of charity work and often

meets with children who consider him a hero. Can you name a well-known personality you have met? What was it like meeting them? Were you a bigger fan of theirs after meeting them?

Chapter 7: Christine Sinclair (1983 -)

"When I was growing up, you didn't know there was a women's national team. Now girls grow up dreaming of playing for Canada." — Christine Sinclair

Country: Canada

Major Teams: Portland Piltos; Vancouver Angels; Vancouver Breakers; Vancouver Whitecaps FC; FC Gold Pride; Western New York Flash; Portland Thorns

Career Span: 1999 - Present

Career Highlights: 2 NCAA Division 1 Women's Soccer Championship titles; 2 Women's Professional Soccer Championship titles; 3 National Women's Soccer League Championship titles; 1 Olympic Gold Medal (2021); Most international goals (men or women—190 goals)

Family Ties

Christine Sinclair was born into a very sporty family. The family's choice of sport had always been soccer. Her father, Bill, and two uncles, Brian and Bruce, all played at a high level and had won many Canadian Championship trophies.

Christine Sinclair (1983 -)

She had a bit of a headstart on the other kids when she started playing for the under-seven team her mom was coaching at the time. The thing that caught the eye of most spectators was that Christine was only four years old! While many of the other kids her age would struggle just to run without tripping over their own feet, Christine was already able to dribble with a ball and take the ball off others. She didn't really like soccer that much, though, as her other friends weren't allowed to play with her.

Christina and her older brother, Mike, loved playing other sports as well. They would often spend their afternoons playing baseball, basketball and soccer inside the family house. Both of them were very competitive, and so they would always go in at each other hard. This competitive streak, unfortunately, had its casualties. Windows, vases, glasses... You name it, it was broken in the Sinclair household due to either a sporting incident or a scuffle that resulted from the incidents.

The brother and sisterly bond was strong, though. Christine and Mike were often grounded when they would fight or break something. Each would be sent to their respective rooms to serve time outs. While their parents thought the kids were being left alone to think about what they did. Usually either Christine or Mike would climb out of their bedroom window and into the other's bedroom via the window.

From this very young age, both siblings always felt it would be better to go through tough times together. It was an important lesson that she would carry with her through her playing career. Not that there were many players she didn't get along with, but during tough times, she always knew she and her teammates could rely on each other.

By the time she was a teenager, soccer was her sport of choice. She made her under-14 provincial team and decided to drop all the other sports that had been taking up all her time. Her coach also saw great potential in her and told her as much. He reckoned she would be playing for the national team in a few years. He was wrong, though, as it didn't take a few years. At age 15, Christine was first chosen to represent Canada!

Leader Among Women

Sinclair had a cracker of a start to her international career. She scored goals at an unprecedented rate, helping Canada become a force to be reckoned with. They often finished in the top four teams at these tournaments but never quite managed to win.

Sinclair quickly built up a reputation for not only her on-the-field heroics but also for being one of the most likable players off the

Christine Sinclair (1983 -)

field. While she had become something of a celebrity in her home country, she never let it go to her head. The coaches and management also respected her, and when the team needed to choose a new captain in 2006, no one batted an eye when the 23-year-old Sinclair was selected.

Sinclair continued to show that she was willing to risk it all for her country, including famously finishing a match despite her nose being elbowed out of joint and broken. Inspired by her gutsy performances, Canada finally saw success in 2011 when they won the Gold Medal at the Pan American Games. Going into the 2012 London Olympics, there was great hope for the Canadians.

Sinclair led the charge as the team progressed to the knockout stages. They beat the host nation, Great Britain, with Sinclair adding to her tally of goals in the tournament. In the semifinals, Canada would play the U.S.A.

As she had done so often, Sinclair scored the first goal in the 22nd minute. The U.S. then equalized, but the Canadians once again took the courtesy of Sinclair. The U.S. once again managed to draw level a few minutes later. The crowd sensed that they were witnessing something that would be talked about for years to come.

Sinclair must have thought that she secured the victory when she completed her hattrick with 17 minutes to play and put the Canadians ahead again. A questionable refereeing decision saw a series of events that saw the U.S. ladies equalizing again. The match ended up going to extra time. With no further goals scored, it looked like the match would go to penalties. There would be one final twist, though, when the U.S. scored in time added on to win the match and knock the Canadians out.

The Canadians were fuming and saddened. They believed they had been the best team on the day, and only the referee's decision cost them a spot in the final.

Sinclair entered the locker room after that game, and the only sound she heard was her teammates sobbing. She threw her cleats down. "She said something like, 'Keep your heads up, I love this team, we've got a bronze medal to win, and I'm not leaving here without one,'" Tancredi says. Sinclair remembers saying this, too: "I've never been prouder to be on a field with a team." And there might've been a bit of swearing.

Herdman stood outside the locker room with the team's sports psychologist, carefully crafting the message he'd give his squad. Glass came out with a tear in her eye and told him, don't bother: "Christine said it all." "It wouldn't have mattered what I said or anyone else," Herdman reflects. "She's got the biggest influence

Christine Sinclair (1983 -)

on this group of women." Says Tancredi: "That was the lowest moment in our careers, and to hear your captain come in, tears in her eyes, and freakin' yelling that? That's why when she speaks, you listen." Canada won the bronze medal two days later. Sinclair isn't in a lot of on-field celebration pictures because she was lying on the grass, bawling.

Creating Her Story

The world had been thrown into turmoil in 2020 due to the spread of the COVID-19 virus. This affected just about everyone, and even the planned Tokyo Olympics were postponed by a year. Sinclair was by now reaching the end of her illustrious career, and when the discussions as to who was the greatest female player of all time came up, one black mark that critics often held against her was the fact that she had never won an international tournament. She had already become the all-time leading goalscorer in international women's soccer; going into these Olympic games, many were wondering if she could finally manage to bring home an Olympic Gold Medal for Canada.

They would have to have their work cut out for them. They would be playing the hosts, Japan, in the opening match. In a tournament with group stages, there is huge pressure to not lose the opening match. The fact that crowds were not allowed to attend due to the ongoing pandemic must have helped a bit, as the Canadians would not have to contend with over 40,000 Japanese fans. The tournament got off to a dream start for Sinclair, who was playing her 300th match for Canada when he netted a goal six minutes into play. Unfortunately for the Canadians, the Japanese drew level six minutes before the end of play, and the match ended in a draw.

Canada would progress to the knockout stages after beating Chile and playing to a one-all draw with Great Britain. They would come up against Brazil in the quarterfinals. The match ended goalless, and after extra time, the teams were forced to line up for penalties. The veteran Sinclair was first up. The unthinkable happened when she couldn't convert. Disappointed as she was, she had to remind herself that it was a team sport. If one player has a bad day, there are still ten other players to pick things up. And pick things up they did, as the remaining four Canadian penalties were all converted to send them through to the semifinals against their biggest rivals and tournament favorites, the U.S.A.

Sinclair also chatted with her coach after the match. Due to the respect she had gained over the years, her opinion had become one of the most entrusted. She told the coach that she believed

Christine Sinclair (1983 -)

one of the younger players, Jessie Fleming, had been showing some promise during training for penalties. Although she was considered the greatest goal scorer in the history of the women's game, she felt that Fleming should be taking penalties in the future (Sinclair & Brunt, 2022).

This would come to play an instrumental role in the rest of the tournament. The rematch of the 2012 semifinal was again a tight one, with very little to choose from between the teams. There were fewer goals this time around, with the score still tied at nil-nil with fifteen minutes to play. A penalty was then awarded to Canada. Sinclair picked up the ball and personally delivered it to Fleming; in a moment, many saw it as a passing of the torch. Fleming converted the penalty to send the Canadians ahead. With the supporters back home on the edge of their seats, they managed to hold on to book their place in the finals!

Sinclair knew that this would probably be her last chance at winning an Olympic Gold Medal, and with the pandemic continuing to put countries in lockdowns every few months, the world wasn't even sure how much soccer there would be played in the upcoming years. It was now or never for Sinclair.

Canada came up against Sweden in the final. The Swedes took the lead in the first half. Canada tried hard but just could not break through the Swedish defence. We can only imagine the rousing speech Sinclair must have given at halftime. "Ladies. I have been representing Canada for over 20 years now. I have never played with a team this strong, and we simply can't let this opportunity slip. This is probably my last opportunity, and I refuse to go down without a fight! Who's with me?" The team roared. So many times, she had proven to be the spark that lit the fire under her team, and this game would be no different.

In the second half, Sinclair won a penalty for Canada. The eyes of the world were once again on her. Again, as she had told the coach a few matches earlier, she handed the ball to Fleming. Fleming slotted the penalty to draw the scores level. As many suspected, Sinclair's body just could not handle another bout of extra time, and so she was substituted.

The match eventually went to penalties, and the Canadians again came out tops. They had done it! Christine Sinclair's Canada had finally won the Olympic Gold Medal! It was Canada's greatest soccer triumph, and many considered it the greatest possible thank you that the Canadian soccer team, some of whom were born after Sinclair made her national debut, could repay her. After the match, most of the players were in tears. Many of the players interviewed afterward pointed out that the victory felt so surreal, and they were most proud to have won the medal

Christine Sinclair (1983 -)

alongside their girlhood hero (Squizzato, 2021). Canadian soccer was in good hands, built on the foundation of Christine Sinclair.

Her legacy cemented, Sinclair would retire in 2023, having given it her all for her country for well over 20 years. She retired as the second most-capped player in internationals and the all-time leading international goalscorer. There is a good reason why many consider her one of the greatest players to ever grace the soccer field.

Activities

1. Christine Sinclair's first coach was her mom. Who was your first or favorite sports coach? What were some of the important lessons or things they taught you?

2. Christine Sinclair and her brother were often grounded for breaking things in their house. She now knows that if she weren't punished, they would never learn their lesson. Were you ever grounded or punished for a similar incident? What lesson did you learn from this?

3. Christine Sinclair was known as a team player who would always put the team ahead of herself. What qualities do you look for in great teammates?

Chapter 8:
Marta (1986 -)

Marta (1986 -)

"I remember I suffered a lot of discrimination and prejudice. My family didn't approve. They didn't accept it because people still thought that girls weren't allowed to play soccer." — Marta

Country: Brazil

Major Teams: Vasco da Gama; Santa Cruz; Umea IK; Los Angeles Sol; Santos; Gold Pride; Western New York Flash; Tyreso; Rosengard; Orlando Pride

Career Span: 2000 - Present

Career Highlights: 7 Damallsvenskan titles; 1 Svenska Cupen title; 1 UEFA Women's Cup; 1 Copa Libertadores de Futbol title; 2 Women's Professional Soccer titles; 6 FIFA Women's Player of the Year awards; 1 FIFA Women's World Cup Golden Boot and Golden Ball (2007) awards; FIFA Women's World Cup all-time record goalscorer; # 7 in Sports Illustrated Top 20 Female Athletes of the Decade (2000-2009)

But She's a Girl?

Ask any boy who grew up in the past twenty years to name the greatest Brazilian soccer player of their generation, and you'll almost certainly hear names like Ronaldo, Ronaldinho, Rivaldo, Roberto Carlos, Coutinho, Kaka, and Neymar mentioned over and over again. One name that should be at the top of everyone's list, though, is often forgotten about.

Marta da Silva is arguably her country's greatest player after Pele, yet because she is a woman, few outside Brazil or followers of the women's game have even heard of her name. With the equality movement in soccer, which she has played a massive role in, making great strides, this is bound to change in the coming years and decades.

Her story starts as so many have for the greatest soccer players to come from Brazil. Her father left her mother and the kids when she was still a baby. This meant that her mother was responsible for raising her and her three brothers all by herself. The family, like so many others outside Brazil's main cities, fell into the poverty trap. The children would often go to bed hungry; they often skipped school because there was no one to make sure they went, and they had to go without what many others consider necessities. Her mother worked hard to give the children what little she could afford, and for the young Marta, this was the only inspiration she needed. She knew that one day, she would make something of herself so that she could repay her mom for all she did for her.

Marta (1986 -)

She first tried to start playing soccer when she started school. Unlike anyone else in this book, you read that correctly. Tried, because when she wanted to join her brothers and their friends in street soccer matches, she was told, "Marta, go sit down! Girls can't play soccer." She would argue with them, "Why are you scared that a girl could play better than you?" Some of the other boys would shout, "Oooh," as if to ridicule the young girl for even daring to think that she belonged on the same "field" as them. The brothers would sometimes give in and let her play, often with a caveat, "Fine, but if you get hurt, it's your own fault." Sometimes, some of the other boys, perhaps fearing that they would be embarrassed, would refuse to play if a girl was allowed to play with them.

Marta, however, was unintimidated and unwavering. She tried to join the local boys' team but faced opposition. The family was still struggling, and Marta's mom couldn't afford to buy her soccer boots. Marta, luckily, had no problem playing barefoot. So-called supporters on the side of the field were ruthless and relentless.

"Booo!" (Whenever she would get the ball)

"Hey, girl! Get off the field!"

"Coach, take that girl off! Soccer is for boys only!"

"What are you going to do? Go home and cry like a girl?" (After being tackled)

"She doesn't even have boots! Take her off the field!"

The negativity wasn't reserved for Marta alone. Her mother and grandmother would also be on the receiving end of these comments.

"Lady, you should be ashamed of yourself. Allowing your little girl to play soccer. What kind of example are you setting?"

"Soccer is a boys' sport. Go home, take your girl with you, and buy her a doll."

While many would have been put off and mentally broken by these taunts, Marta felt lucky enough to have her mother and grandmother on the sidelines supporting her during every match. Besides, her mother was too busy trying to make enough money to put food on the table to be bothered by these silly comments. The nasty comments made Marta mentally strong, as she absolutely loved showing off exactly why the coach put her on the team.

However, there were sometimes factors outside her control. She and her team faced further obstacles when they would sometimes pitch up to matches, and the opposition coach would

Marta (1986 -)

refuse to have his team take the field if they were playing against a girl. This even happened in some championship matches, as the opposition coaches cited the fine print in the rules (da Silva, 2019). Marta, however, just wanted to play soccer. She didn't see what the big deal was. If she was good enough to play, why couldn't she? After all, nothing pleased her more than being able to contribute to her team's successes.

On to Rio

When she turned 14, many outside of her family started to encourage her to consider making soccer her career. It was something of a radical idea in Brazil. Women's soccer was definitely not on the same level as the men's game. Worse still, it was not even on the same level as other countries that had women's leagues. While there were very few options, Marta was told the absolute worst would be to remain where she was.

She learned that there was an opportunity waiting for her in Rio de Janeiro. The coaches at Vasco de Gama wished to see what all this fuss was about with this girl who played among the boys. Marta battled with the idea of leaving her family, friends and her team behind. She was also petrified because the big cities were very different from the village she grew up in. The big cities were a lot more liberal, and no one batted an eye when a girl played soccer. On the converse, she had never been in one of these cities for a long time, let alone by herself. She knew it would be a very tough adjustment, but she also knew she had to be brave not only for her sake but also for the sake of her family.

She was only 14, but she decided to take the opportunity and packed her bags with what little clothing she had. She was almost penniless and wasn't sure if the life waiting for her in Rio would be any better than the one she was currently living. She nonetheless bought the bus ticket that she hoped would be her ticket to a better life. It took all of three days for the bus to arrive in Rio, but she had made it.

On the day of her trial, she immediately impressed former Brazilian players who were now the coaches. She dribbled past player after player with ease and seemed to score goals at will. The staff didn't mess about and signed her up despite her young age. They were convinced that they had just seen the start of something spectacular (Simplicio, 2019).

From there, things moved fast for Marta. By her own admission, the period seemed like a bit of a whirlwind. Within three years, she was chosen to represent Brazil for the first time at age 16. She then took a huge leap of faith and moved to Sweden to play

Marta (1986 -)

for Umea IK. She soon became one of the most talked-about players in all of women's soccer due to her goal-scoring prowess. In 2006, she was rewarded for her remarkable performances when FIFA voted her its Player of the Year, an award that she would win for the next four years straight.

She decided to return home to share the award with her family. Despite arriving back home at almost midnight, she could not believe her eyes when the entire town came out to welcome her. It is often said that Brazil loves a winner, and this was certainly proof of that. The fire department had even come out so that she could sit atop the truck and be seen. Quite the turnaround from just 10 years earlier when some of the same people fought tooth and nail to keep her out of soccer.

It was at this moment Marta realized that her football career had to be dedicated to more than just herself. She was not only playing for herself or even the girls standing waving in front of her that night. Her actions on the soccer field could be used to inspire young girls all around the world! Since then, it has been exactly that thought that she continues to take to the field for every match.

Marta—The Female Pele (Or Better?)

Over the coming years, Marta would go on to break nearly every record in women's football. She led Brazil to win eight out of the nine Copa America championships held to date and won league titles wherever she went, almost always finishing top goal scorer for the season.

She would also go on to break records. She became Brazil's most prolific goal scorer ever, man or woman, and was voted FIFA's Player of the Year an unprecedented six times, with the next most wins by one player being three times.

If you ask Marta, though, nothing on the field will ever compare to what she has achieved off it. On the soccer field, she became known as a great leader. She also transitioned off the field to a great leader and motivational speaker.

She became involved with the United Nations as a Nations Development Programme Goodwill Ambassador in 2010 and, subsequently, a U.N. Women's Goodwill Ambassador. She continues to speak on equality issues, providing girls around the world with hope for a more equal future in not only sport but also life—an equal future that did not seem possible for her when she was growing up. She is also often chosen as a FIFA ambassador,

Marta (1986 -)

most notably for their Live Your Goals Campaign.

Marta is admittedly reaching the end of her career and is already thinking toward the future of Brazil soccer. After Brazil was knocked out of the 2019 FIFA Women's World Cup, Marta gained worldwide recognition for an interview she gave. The post-match interview is often cited as one of the greatest in not only soccer, or even women's soccer, but in all sports. She looked into the camera and spoke directly to the young girls of Brazil, "It's wanting more. It's training more. It's taking care of yourself more. It's being ready to play 90 plus 30 minutes. This is what I ask of the girls... The women's game depends on you to survive, So think about that. Value it more. Cry in the beginning so you can smile in the end." She was reminding girls that there won't always be a Marta on the field and that the fight for equal rights will continue after she's retired (Carroll, 2019).

She is now undoubtedly one the greatest players to take to the soccer field. Her records might one day fall, but her legendary status for her on-the-field exploits, as well as her philanthropic exploits off the field, continue to inspire both boys and girls around the world.

Activities

1. **Marta had to learn from an early age that not everyone**

was happy to have boys and girls playing together. Have you or someone you know ever not been allowed to take part in an activity? Why were you (or the other person) not allowed to take part? Do you feel this was unfair, and could you (or the other person) eventually take part?

2. Marta was forced to move away from home at a very early age. She was very scared at first, but eventually, things worked out for her. Can you describe a risky situation that scared you at first but that you eventually overcame? How did you overcome the situation?

3. Marta is very involved with FIFA's Live Your Goals campaign. What are three goals you want to achieve in soccer? How do you plan to achieve each of these goals?

Chapter 9:
Cristiano Ronaldo
(1983 -)

"Dreams are not what you see in your sleep; dreams are things which do not let you sleep." — Cristiano Ronaldo

Country: Portugal

Major Teams: Sporting Lisbon; Manchester United; Real Madrid; Juventus; Al Nassr

Career Span: 2002 - Present

Career Highlights: 3 Premier League titles; 1 FA Cup; 2 La Liga titles; 2 Copa del Rey titles; 5 UEFA Champions League titles; 2 Serie A titles; 1 Coppa Italie title; 1 Arab Club Champions Cup; 1 UEFA European Championship (2016); 5 FIFA Ballon d'Or awards; 1 FIFA Puskas Award.

Ronaldo #2

"*Siuuu*!" A celebration that has become part of pop culture beyond just soccer. Even the most casual of fans will be able to associate the run, aerial spin, landing with outstretched arms, and shouting, "siuuu," with Cristiano Ronaldo.

Ronaldo's road to becoming one of the greatest players of all time was a rocky one. He was born into an impoverished family,

Cristiano Ronaldo (1983 -)

sharing a room with his three siblings. He started playing soccer at a local club where his father was an equipment manager (Rolin, 2019). By the time he was a teenager, he was a troubled student. He was performing poorly at school and was known to have a temper. His inability to control his temper eventually saw him expelled from school.

His soccer career was blossoming, though, as he was playing semi-professionally. At this young age, the young Ronaldo took a big gamble. It's not one he encourages other kids to do, but he felt at the time he had no choice. He decided to drop out of school in the sixth grade (EFE, 2017).

A year later, when he was 15, Ronaldo faced another hurdle when he was diagnosed with a heart condition. He was told he needed surgery, or otherwise, it would likely be the end of his soccer career. For Ronaldo, it was an easy decision. Without soccer, he had nothing and so would get the surgery. The surgery was a success. He made a swift and full recovery and was back on the soccer field within no time. There was no stopping him now. Within years, he found himself in the Sporting Lisbon first-team locker room and then made the big move to Manchester United in England.

Throughout his initial rise in the mid-1990s through the early-

2000s, the best player in the world was arguably a Brazilian striker called Ronaldo. The world could never have imagined that by the time his career was done a few years later, he would be the second-most famous Ronaldo. That, however, is exactly what happened in the coming years.

"Talent Without Hard Work is Nothing"

Cristiano Ronaldo is often cited as one of, if not the hardest-working players to have ever graced the soccer field. In the "Messi vs Ronaldo" debate, you won't find many who will claim that Ronaldo was the more naturally gifted of the two. While definitely not saying that Messi doesn't work hard, it is a general consensus among soccer experts that Ronaldo had to work a little harder to even come close to challenging Messi in the battle to be called the best soccer player in the world year upon year.

There is evidence of this from Ronaldo's earliest days at Manchester United. When he signed with them, he was considered to be a diamond in the rough, but the soccer world had seen so many of these diamonds in the rough come and go due to them trying to rely more on talent than putting in the work to craft their skill.

Cristiano Ronaldo (1983 -)

This was before his rivalry with Messi even started. Ronaldo was never just glad to be a part of the team. He wanted to be the best player in the world! He was in a Manchester United team filled with established stars much older than him. He did not let this turn him off, though; he committed to training harder than anyone else.

His extra training has become the stuff of legends. The Manchester United team at the time included such midfield stalwarts like Paul Scholes, Nicky Butt, and Ryan Giggs, alongside such promising youngsters like Kleberson, Eric Djemba-Djemba, Duncan Fletcher, and Quinton Fortune. Ronaldo knew he needed something to set himself apart. David Beckham, perhaps the greatest free-kick taker the country and team had ever seen, had just transferred to Real Madrid as Ronaldo was arriving at Manchester United. Ronaldo saw this as the opening he needed to gain the edge on some of the players he would be competing with in the midfield for a place in the starting lineup.

He was lucky to have a great coaching staff consisting of Carlos Queiroz, Mick Phelan, Rene Meulensteen, and the legendary Sir Alex Ferguson. Thankfully for Ronaldo, they had no problem giving in to his requests when he asked them if they could work with him after regular training so that he, too, could learn to master free kicks. There was a typical discussion that would occur almost daily in the Manchester United changing room among teammates.

"Where's Ronaldo?"

"Oh, he's probably still out there practicing his set piece kicks again."

That he was; he was advised to take a step to the side, which would make his approach more natural. The coaching team relished the challenge. They would video-record the sessions and study them with Ronaldo.

The coaches also encouraged him to become more attacking-minded. When he was told to set a target number of goals for one season, Ronaldo answered 23, but the coaching team rebutted with 43. They then worked relentlessly on his positioning on the field, using zones inside the box, and how to create finishing opportunities for himself (Austin, 2017).

To practice his ball control, Ronaldo would look for unconventional methods that didn't require anyone's assistance. The Manchester United training grounds bordered on woodlands, with very uneven grounding due to the tree's routes that would run above ground. He would kick the ball hard into

Cristiano Ronaldo (1983 –)

this area and attempt to bring the bouncing ball under his control (Ambrose, 2017).

One of the biggest changes Ronaldo would see in those early years was to his physique. He arrived at Manchester United and was a bit on the scrawny side. Mick Clegg was the coach Ronaldo worked most closely with to help develop him into the man he would become. Clegg remembers the shy Ronaldo coming up to him when he first joined the club, "Can you please help me become the best player in the world? I want to be better than Giggs. I want to be better than everyone else."

Clegg loved a long-term challenge and devised a program involving strengthening initially, then upper body and core work, which involved a lot of boxing, weights, squats, and jumps. For his reaction speed, there were more boxing drills and the D2 machine in the gym. For foot movement, there were mostly ladders and jump ropes.

As Ronaldo grew in size, so did his on-field ability to overpower opponents. The biggest difference Clegg observed, however, was in Ronaldo's mentality and cognitive development. He went from a player who was easily annoyed and sometimes even got yellow and red cards to one of the steeliest and calmest minds in all of soccer (Roberts, 2019). A far cry from the boy who was expelled from school years earlier.

It was with this tireless work ethic that Ronaldo eventually rose to become one of the best soccer players in the world. By 2008, he was voted the best player in the world, and he won the Ballon d'Or. It would be the first of many accolades and ultimately saw him becoming the most expensive player in the world (at the time) when he transferred from Manchester United to Real Madrid. The legend of Cristiano Ronaldo would only grow on to grow and grow over the coming years.

Obrigado, Ronaldo!

Portugal had long been considered the greatest European soccer giant to have never won a title. They were among the favorites to win the 1966 World Cup when the great Eusebio was at the height of his powers. Much was also expected from what was dubbed the "Golden Generation." Future legends like Luis Figo and Rui Costa formed the base for the early 1990s Portuguese youth team that won the under-21 World Cup, and they were expected to bring home either a World Cup or European Championship. Unfortunately, they were never able to, with 2004 runners-up being their best finish.

Cristiano Ronaldo (1983 -)

A young, 19-year-old Ronaldo had been a part of that 2004 squad. The whole of Portugal was heartbroken when they lost in the final to Greece in what is considered one of the biggest upsets in all of soccer history. The tournament was being held in Portugal, and many had predicted a fairytale ending for many of the aforementioned Golden Generation.

By the following Euro tournament, Ronaldo was already captaining Portugal, but the team's results never improved on their previous Euro final. They performed well in World Cups and Euros but would always get knocked out in the knockout stages. In the 2014 World Cup, they failed to make it out of their group, and some experts predicted that this was the end of Ronaldo's chances of ever winning an international tournament.

By the time Euro 2016 rolled around, Portugal was no longer considered the powerhouse it once was, with many players who were considered past their prime mixed in with inexperienced players. The team was generally considered to be Ronaldo plus ten other players. While Ronaldo loved his teammates, he knew the country's chances of winning rested squarely on his shoulders.

Portugal scraped through the group stages, only qualifying for the knockout phases as a best-placed third finisher. Ronaldo contributed with goals, assists, and converting a vital penalty in Portugal's march toward the final against France. The French were favorites to take the cup in front of their home crowd, but this was not the first time Ronaldo's back was up against the wall.

There was to be a major plot twist. Early in the match, Ronaldo was tackled and looked to be struggling to get up. "Come on, it can't end this way," he must have told himself as he tried to run it off. Ten minutes later, the pain in his knee had not gone away. He left the field briefly to get his knee strapped. He came back out, but it was clear something was very wrong. He went down in tears, as did many of his and Portugal's supporters, and had to be stretchered off the field. To the many who believed that Portugal was a one-man team, the match was as good as done.

Ronaldo, however, believed in his teammates. The Portuguese held on, as the now heavily favored French team failed to put the ball in the net. They came close a number of times, even putting the ball into the net in a heart-stopping moment two minutes into injury time. The match would then go to extra time. Ronaldo felt powerless; one can only imagine the mental anguish he must have been going through, knowing he was supposed to play the lead role that night.

Cristiano Ronaldo (1983 -)

The scores remained deadlocked at the end of the first half of extra time. Early into the second half, the impossible happened. Eder scored to give Portugal the lead. Despite bringing on attacking substitutes, France was unable to draw level. When the whistle blew, Portugal, after all these years, had finally won their first international title!

When it was time for the trophy presentation, captain Ronaldo hobbled up to accept the cup. There was, after all, no other player who deserved this honor more than the man who had made this moment possible.

CR7—The Greatest?

Ronaldo has become one of the most recognizable soccer players and athletes of the modern generation. His crafted brand of CR7 (after the number he wore through most of his career) only increased his celebrity. He has not only won just about every domestic trophy in every country he ever played in but has also been featured in magazine lists like ESPN, Forbes, and Time, not to mention the Guinness Book of World Records.

He has also contributed his time and resources to charities around the world. Some of the more noteworthy causes he has supported included funding a cancer center in his hometown (where his mother had received treatment) and supporting the plight of refugees.

Ronaldo's sheer drive to become one of the best players in the world, as well as the cultural symbol he has become, has and will continue to inspire younger players across the world.

Activities

1. Ronaldo is known as one of the hardest-working players to ever play soccer. Can you recall something you really wanted to become good at? What hard work did you put into making this goal a reality?

2. Fitness has always been an aspect that has set Ronaldo apart. How would you describe your fitness? What exercises do you do to keep fit?

3. Ronaldo started his international career playing with some of the greatest soccer players his country ever saw. Who are five of the greatest players who have played for your country? What made them great?

Chapter 10:
Lionel Messi (1987 -)

"When you lose, you get up, you make mistakes, and you learn.

And then you become a better player" —Lionel Messi

Country: Argentina

Major Teams: Barcelona; Paris Saint-Germain; Inter Miami

Career Span: 2003 - Present

Career Highlights: 10 La Liga titles; 7 Copa del Rey titles; 4 UEFA Champions League titles; 2 Ligue 1 titles; 1 FIFA World Cup (2022); 8 FIFA Ballon d'Or awards; 2 FIFA World Cup Gold Ball awards; 2 Laureus World Sportsman of the Year awards

It's Not About How Big You Are; It's About How Big You Play

Lionel Messi was born into a soccer-crazy family. He started playing soccer almost as soon as he was old enough to walk. He was often invited to play by his two older brothers, cousins, and their friends. Growing up, Leo, as he was known to most, was always a bit shorter than the other kids his age. This did not, however, stop him from taking part in his favorite activity, playing soccer. His father was also a soccer coach at the local club, so it was to the surprise of no one when Leo joined the club at age four (Adan, 2022)

Lionel Messi (1987 -)

His natural talent was evident early on, but unfortunately, so was his short stature. His grandmother was his biggest supporter as a boy. She would attend all his training sessions and matches. When the time came for Leo to finally play competitive matches, the coaches left him on the bench, believing him to be too small to play. His grandmother attended the match and watched as the team struggled.

Leo's team went two goals down, and his grandmother couldn't keep her mouth shut anymore. "Bring Leo on!" The coaches responded, "No! He is too small. The other players will eat him alive." "Nonsense," replied his grandmother, "He'll show you. Put him on the field, and he'll save the match!" The annoyed coaches eventually gave in and put Leo on. In a sign of things to come, he scored two goals quickly to help his team draw the match. That day, Leo pointed to his grandmother every time he scored a goal to say thank you for believing in him. His grandmother would pass away a few years later, but that has not stopped him from still thanking her after every goal he scores by pointing to the heavens.

He continued to be teased for his height all through his junior years. He always responded with the same attitude his grandma had, "I'll show them!" He happened to see a poster one day that featured what would go on to become his go-to motivation whenever he took the field. "*It's not about how big you are; it's about how big you play.*" And there was no "*bigger*" player on the field whenever Leo was on it. Until age 10, he scored an incredible 234 goals in 176 matches for the Newell's Old Boys.

There were both more problems and opportunities that soon lay ahead. When he was nine years old, it looked like Leo had completely stopped growing. Doctors soon found out he had a growth problem and advised his parents to start a very expensive treatment as soon as possible, as leaving it untreated could lead to more serious problems for Leo in the future. The treatment involved daily hormone injections.

His club decided they would try to help pay for the treatment, but they soon realized this would not be possible. While he was at first scared and sad, Messi soon just thought of it as normal. Some people wear glasses to help them see, others have to use creams to treat skin conditions, and others take daily medication to help them treat conditions. For Leo, this quickly became the norm, and he even began figuring out how to inject himself without the help of his parents.

The treatment seemed to be working, but the family had come to realize they would struggle to continue paying for it. When he was 12 years old, Leo's father devised a plan based on his

Lionel Messi (1987 -)

previous experience—he would try to use Leo's soccer abilities to get him signed with one of the best clubs in the world and have them pay for the treatment. It was a long shot, but he somehow managed to have a scout pass along a positive review to Barcelona.

Barcelona was interested in seeing Leo's talents up close and invited him to join them for training on a trial basis. "He's the next Diego Maradona! You simply must sign him," is what the Barcelona management was told. "Oh boy. Here we go again," would have been the response from every member of the management team, who had probably seen dozens of the "*next Pele*" and the "*next Maradonas*" (referring to soccer-playing youth players from Brazil and Argentina, respectively) pass through their youth system over the years.

Leo, his father, and his agent arrived at Barcelona for the tryout, and the other players in the youth team, which included future legends Cesc Fabregas and Gerard Pique, could not believe how small he was. The young Leo quietly reminded himself, "It's not about how big you are; it's about how big you play." He went out and showed the management what all the hype was about, with the team deciding within two minutes to sign him.

Famously, a deal was put together so quickly that Barcelona had the young Leo sign on a napkin. Barcelona didn't want word to get out of their new prospect or risk losing him to another team. They agreed on everything Leo and his parents wanted. This included relocating the entire family to Barcelona and paying for Leo's growth hormone treatment. Messi's journey to becoming one of the greatest players the world has ever seen was now in full swing (Lowe, 2014).

La Pulga Strikes

Messi would go on to successfully treat his condition and would grow to the height of a normal adult. He would quickly rise through the youth ranks at Barcelona. He was known for being quiet among his teammates and preferred for his performances on the field do the talking. Due to his size and perhaps how swiftly he annoyed the opposition, he was given the nickname *La Pulga* (Spanish for The Flea).

He made his full-team debut for Barcelona in the 2004/05 season at age 17 and was first chosen for Argentina in 2005. His first season at Barcelona signaled a prophetic turning of the tide. They won the league for the first time in six seasons. Although he showed significant promise, Messi struggled to cement his spot in what was considered by many to be a World XI-caliber

Lionel Messi (1987 -)

team of established stars.

By the end of the decade, though, Barcelona had sold some of their high-profile players, and Messi had become their best player, averaging nearly a goal per game. He was also rewarded for his stellar 2009 with his first Ballon d'Or Award. This award is handed out annually to the world's best soccer player. Not even Messi could have envisioned what a huge part this award would play in his life. If they were to ever rename this award in honor of a soccer player, it would almost certainly be Messi. He has managed to win this award a record eight times, including four consecutive years, since first winning it!

Crowning Moment

By 2022, Messi had won just about every award and trophy he had ever played for: the La Liga in Spain, the Ligue 1 in France, the UEFA Champions League, league cups, and even an Olympic Gold Medal. The one trophy missing from his collection was the FIFA World Cup. He was on a long list of players whose lack of international success was used against them when debating who the greatest players of all time were.

Messi had played in four World Cup tournaments since 2006.

While they always performed well, Argentina's best finish since their glory years was finishing runners-up to Germany in 2014 in Brazil. Many were starting to question if Argentina would ever again manage to win a World Cup, as they couldn't even win a *Copa America* trophy. After missing a penalty in the 2015 final, Messi faced harsh and unjust criticism from Argentina's fanbase. As a result, Messi decided to retire. Many saw this as the final blow to Argentina ever again winning a World Cup (or anytime soon, at least).

Messi had a change of heart and announced his return to international soccer just in time for the 2018 World Cup qualifiers. He captained Argentina for the campaign and inspired the team in his own special way. As always, he focused more on the on-field action than the off-the-field shenanigans. They managed to qualify for the 2018 World Cup but couldn't progress beyond the Round of 16 — losing to France in a thrilling 4-3 encounter.

By 2021, many were speculating whether age wasn't starting to catch up with Messi. He wasn't scoring quite as many domestic goals as he used to and was also nearing the age at which most players start thinking about retirement. Many critics felt that the upcoming *Copa America* and World Cup tournaments would be Messi's last chance to right the many wrongs he had

Lionel Messi (1987 –)

experienced at these tournaments over the past nearly 20 years.

Messi answered these doubters the way he had his entire career, by putting in inspiring performances. Argentina would go on to win their first *Copa America* title in nearly 20 years with Messi playing a crucial role, finishing as the joint top goal scorer and the player of the tournament.

The following year it was the World Cup. It would likely be Messi's last, and his final opportunity to write his place in the record books. Very few players in any sport ever get the opportunity to cap their careers off with the biggest prize in their sport. Messi would be attempting this.

The Argentine team got off to a shaky start. Despite an early penalty by Messi, they would suffer a shock 2-1 defeat to Saudi Arabia. This almost certainly meant Argentina had to win each of their remaining matches in the tournament if they were to win the trophy. Not many gave them a chance, but Messi had faced worse odds before in his career. Messi scored again in the second half of the next match, and teammate Enzo doubled their lead to keep the team's hopes alive. They would beat Poland in the final group stage match 2-0 to secure their place in the knockout stages.

Messi would continue to play the tournament of his life in the knockout stages, scoring in the Round of 16 en route to Argentina, beating Australia 2-1 to progress to the quarterfinals. In an ill-tempered match against the Netherlands, Messi again scored his team's second goal. They led 2-0 going into the final 10 minutes, but the Dutch managed to score in the 83rd minute and again 11 minutes into injury time to force extra time and, ultimately, a penalty shootout. Messi converted his penalty, as did three of his teammates, to send Argentina through to the semifinals.

The Argentines came up against Croatia, and Messi once again led from the front. He converted the team's penalty in the first half. He rallied the team together in the second half, as they scored two more goals to send the team through to the finals! Could this be it? Would Messi finally be able to win the big one?

The final would see Argentina play France. Much was made about the battle between two Paris Saint Germain forwards, Lionel Messi for Argentina and Kylian Mbappe for France. France were the defending champions, and Argentina was, more than anything else, looking to give Messi the perfect send-off.

One can only imagine the weight on Messi's shoulders. He was born in 1987, a year after Argentina had last won the World Cup. There was by now a whole generation of soccer fans who had

Lionel Messi (1987 -)

never seen their country lift the World Cup. He must have been thinking of how the little Leo from Rosario could never have imagined that he was now standing on the verge of history. Little could he, or any of the other players involved in the match, have known that they would be involved in one of the greatest matches the soccer world would ever see.

The tension was at a fever pitch, with billions watching around the world. All eyes were on Messi, and the first action of the day was a familiar sight. Messi converted a penalty to put Argentina ahead in the 23rd minute. Many wondered how Messi had remained so confident as to take so many penalties through the tournament and not miss one. He clearly had no fear or lingering memories from the 2015 *Copa America* penalty miss. Angel di Maria put the Argentines 2-0 up in the 36th minute. Going into halftime, Messi just knew the team could not allow this opportunity to slip.

The teams came out for the second half, and with 10 minutes to go, most thought the Argentines had finally secured the cup. France was awarded a penalty in the 80th minute, and Messi's Paris Saint Germain teammate Mbappe converted. A minute later, Mbappe scored again to level the score 2-2. The World Cup Finals had traditionally been known as boring and dull affairs. This one was anything but. The teams were level after the 90 minutes plus injury time, and extra time was next.

Extra time would deliver more action. While many questioned whether the aging Messi should not have been substituted to make way for fresh legs, Messi, of course, would never have deserted his team at this crucial juncture. And if there was any doubt, Messi, as always, led from the front. He scored in the 108th minute to put Argentina ahead once again. Surely, this would be it. Surely, this would finally be the goal to win Argentina the cup. With one hand on the cup and less than three minutes to play, France was awarded another penalty. Messi and the world could not believe it! Mbappe converted the penalty to complete his hat trick and forced the match into a penalty shootout.

France would take the first penalty, and Mbappe converted his. Messi played the role of captain courageously by taking the all-important first penalty. As he had done with each one so far in the tournament, he would convert it to give his team the best possible start. 1-1. France missed both of their next two penalties, while Argentina scored. The French would score one more, but if Argentina successfully converted their next one, they would be champions.

Gonzalo Montiel stepped up to the box. Messi turned his head

Lionel Messi (1987 –)

skyward. "It could be today, Grandma," he whispered to himself (Mukherjee, 2023). Even while standing on the grandest stage, Messi never forgot who gave him his start, his grandma. Montiel would convert his penalty, and Messi and the Argentina team had done it! Argentina was, finally, world champion once again!

While the picture of Messi kissing the trophy was all over the news within minutes, and despite him being the winning captain, winning both the Golden Ball for being the player of the tournament, he was quick to correct journalists who would say Messi won the World Cup. He has maintained and will always maintain that soccer is a team sport. Without the team, there is no Messi.

For his humility in the face of his unprecedented accomplishments on and off the field, Messi remains an inspirational figure not only to millions of kids around the world who see him as the greatest soccer player of his generation but also to all those who believe in leading in a quiet and impactful manner. His story is not yet complete, as he believes he still has a few years left in him.

Activities

1. **Lionel Messi's greatest supporter was his grandmother.** Who are the people you consider your biggest

supporters? What do they do to support you?

2. Lionel Messi had to deal with some teasing when he was younger due to his height. Have you ever had to endure teasing due to your physical appearance? How did you deal with this?

3. Lionel Messi is known for being able to remain calm under pressure. Can you describe a situation where you needed to remain calm while under pressure? Did the situation turn out better because you were able to remain calm than if you had panicked?

Chapter 11:
Neymar (1992 -)

"The secret is to believe in your dreams; in your potential that you can be like your star, keep searching, keep believing and don't lose faith in yourself." —Neymar

Country: Brazil

Major Teams: Santos; Barcelona; Paris Saint Germain; Al Hilal

Career Span: 2009 - Present

Career Highlights: 1 Copa do Brasil; 2 La Liga titles; 3 Copa del Rey titles; 1 UEFA Champion's League; 5 Ligue 1 titles; 3 Coupe de France titles; FIFA Puskas Award (2011)

As Long As There Is a 1% Chance, We Will Have 99% Faith

The soccer player the world would come to know as Neymar Jr has faced adversity almost since the day he was born. His parents struggled to make ends meet. His father worked while trying to pursue his dreams of becoming a professional soccer player but never progressed beyond amateur status in Brazil's lowest league.

When Neymar Jr was still only four months old, the young family was involved in a horrific car accident. The car was in a state,

Neymar (1992 -)

and while his father at first thought the young baby had been flung from the car, it seems his prayers were answered when baby Neymar was found in the car. He was, unfortunately, in a bad state, drenched in blood from a cut on the head and screaming frantically. He was rushed to the hospital, where the family was assured he would make a full recovery. Even today, one can see why Neymar Jr has always been a man of faith, having lived through this ordeal so early in life. A saying was often used in their household that carried Neymar through many tough times when he grew up. "As long as there is a 1% chance, we will have 99% faith." (Neymar, 2017)

The family continued to struggle after the accident. Neymar Sr had to kiss his soccer career goodbye as he never fully recovered from the accident. After Neymar's sister was born, the family was forced to move in with his grandparents as, by this time, the family was living without electricity.

The area they moved into was one of the worst slums on the outskirts of Sao Paulo. The area was particularly known for its poverty, high crime rate, and drug use. Neymar learned an important lesson early on, as his father could easily have turned to crime in order to feed his family, much like many around him were doing. Instead, Neymar Sr worked 2-3 jobs a week just to provide his family with the basics. And eventually, their situation would improve. Neymar Jr learned the value of hard work during this period. There was no need to take shortcuts that could land you in further trouble (Hendrix, 2016).

Neymar Makes His Mark

Neymar enjoyed playing street soccer with friends as well as *futsal*. He recalls how he would wake up every morning and already couldn't wait for school to be over so that he could play soccer. Futsal is an indoor version of soccer, with five players on each side and played on a hard court.

Neymar credits futsal with teaching him a lot, especially his ability to play the ball in tight spaces, which will come in handy in the future (Neymar, 2016). While the odds, again, may have been against Neymar, his father really believed he was a special talent. The family eventually managed to relocate to a better area and got the young Neymar a trial at a top *futsal* team. He passed the trials and joined the team.

After a few years, he had become one of the top futsal players in the state, and prominent clubs had taken note of the boy's wonder. In 2003, Santos, one of Brazil's most historically successful clubs (and the club of Pele), signed Neymar to a deal

Neymar (1992 -)

to join their youth team. By the time he was 14, his prolific goal-scoring and eye-catching skills had caught the eye of some top European scouts. This included Real Madrid. At the time, many of his Brazilian heroes were playing for the Spanish team, including Ronaldo, Robinho and Roberto Carlos. They invited Neymar to a trial, and he and his father jumped at the opportunity. Unfortunately, it was not to be. Neymar Sr was not happy with the deal offered. The younger Neymar was bitterly disappointed, but he trusted his father's judgment. The deal offered was simply not up to standards. While at the time it didn't make sense to the young boy, he now understands that everything in life happens for a reason at the right time.

He would spend more successful seasons at Santos and finally make the highly anticipated move to Europe in 2013. Barcelona was the club that won out in the end. The rest, as they say, is history! Due to his lucrative contract, Neymar and his family would never have to worry about where their next meal would come from or choose between electricity and school fees.

MSN—Teamwork Makes the Dream Work

Neymar arrived in Barcelona to much fanfare, being presented at the famous Camp Nou to over 50,000 fans. He was walking into a locker room that many considered to be a team worthy of being called a World XI on paper. Expectations were high, too, as their fans expected them to win the La Liga title and the UEFA Champion's League just about every year.

Despite his record of scoring and setting up goals, a starting position in Barcelona's team was not assured. They already had Lionel Messi up front, considered by most experts to be the best player at the time. He was assisted by other top stars like Pedro and Alexis Sanchez. By the end of his first season, Neymar had all but forced his way into the starting lineup, contributing vital goals and assists throughout the season.

The next season would prove to be one that took the Barcelona side from great to legendary. The club signed Luis Suarez, who was also at the time considered to be one of the best strikers in Europe over the previous few seasons. Fans, however, could not wait at the prospect of seeing Messi, Suarez, and Neymar all lining up for the same team. Normally, they would only get to see these kinds of dream combinations on the latest version of PlayStation or Xbox's FIFA. Now, they'd be getting to see it weekly.

The Barcelona faithful weren't prepared for what they would

Neymar (1992 –)

witness over the coming months. The season was a typically tight one, with only Barcelona and Real Madrid really in it. The trio of MSN, as they had come to be known, turned out to be the difference. They scored an incredible 81 goals between them in the league (out of Barcelona's 110 total). This meant that the trio actually scored more goals between the three of them than any other team that season except for Real Madrid. Neymar contributed 22 of those, as he helped Barcelona win the La Liga title that year from Real Madrid by just two points.

Barcelona would achieve more success. They would win the Copa del Rey that year as well, too, meaning they had secured the domestic double. To secure their second-ever treble, Barcelona would need to win their first UEFA Champions League since 2010-11. Barcelona was on fire the entire tournament, and between MSN, they were responsible for most of the dominating performances, scoring 25 goals in 12 matches leading up to the finals. Neymar had contributed nine of those twenty-four goals. In the finals, they would come up against Juventus, who had caused a bit of an upset by beating Barcelona's old rivals, Real Madrid.

In the final, Barcelona were the clear favorites, and they did not disappoint. MSN clearly had their working boots on, as Neymar was involved in setting up the first goal in the 4th minute of the match. This would be the only goal of the first half, as Barcelona took the 1-0 lead going into the second half.

Juventus equalized 10 minutes into the second half. There was another scare for Barcelona, as there was a strong shout for a Juventus penalty. It was not given, but this seemed to light a fire under the MSN collective. Minutes later, Messi's shot was blocked, but Suarez managed to convert the rebound to put Barcelona back in front. The crowds were on the edge of their seats as Neymar managed to score a few minutes later. Unfortunately, this goal was disallowed, as the referee said that he had used his hand. In the final minute of the seven added-on minutes, Neymar managed to break away on the counter and score with the final kick of the match to make the score 3-1 to Barcelona. MSN and Barcelona had done it! They had won the treble! Finishing the season on an unprecedented and record 122 goals!

The teamwork and interplay between these three players was a sight to behold. It is not often that three players who are among the best in the world are all on the same team, and it is even rarer that a manager manages to find a way to play all of them together. In this treble-winning season, Luis Enrique managed to find a way. There is a good argument that this attacking unit during this season was one of, if not the, greatest of all time. And

Neymar (1992 -)

Neymar more than played his role!

Neymar followed up this season with more success at Barcelona and then Paris-Saint Germain (where he officially became the most expensive soccer player ever). He also played an instrumental role in Brazil securing their first-ever Olympic Gold Medal in 2016, in front of their home crowd, and would later go on to become Brazil's all-time leading goal scorer. It is for his canny ability to always overcome the odds, and to come out on top on the other side, no matter where he goes, that Neymar is considered a modern legend.

Activities

1. Neymar was involved in a scary situation when he was still a baby. He and his family have always been great believers that everyone should have faith if there is a chance. Can you recall a situation where you or your favorite team were the underdog/s and managed to turn things around? Describe what role having faith played in you overcoming the odds.

2. Neymar loved playing video games as a kid. What are some of the favorite games you've played? What are some things you feel you've learned by playing these games (e.g., Keeping track of player improvements in a

sports game, problem-solving, cognitive skills, etc.)

3. Lionel Messi, Luis Suarez, and Neymar (MSN) were considered to be among the greatest attacking units in the game's history. What are some factors you believe contribute to making a great team?

Chapter 12:
Kylian Mbappe (1998 -)

"The greatest are an inspiration for all the kids who wake up early in the morning. Everyone watches you, is inspired by you and wants to be you. So, you influence society. That's what being more than an athlete means. I want more kids to have that opportunity. I want everybody to start with the same chance." —Kylian Mbappe

Country: France

Major Teams: Monaco FC; Paris Saint Germain

Career Span: 2015 - Present

Career Highlights: 6 Ligue 1 titles; 3 Coupe de France titles; 1 FIFA World Cup title (2018); 4-time Ligue 1 Player of the Year; 1 FIFA World Cup Golden Boot Award (2022); Knight of the Legion of Honour

Bonding in Bondy

Ask any soccer fan who they expect to be the best soccer player in the world for the next 10 years, and the overwhelming consensus will be Kylian Mbappe. His rise was meteoric, and, in a rare case, he has actually surpassed the hype and fulfilled the promise that was attached to his name.

Kylian Mbappe (1998 -)

Things weren't always easy for Kylian, though. He was born into a sporting family; his father was a soccer coach, and his mother was a handball player. France was in the middle of soccer fever. Kylian was born a few months after France had won the World Cup for the first time as hosts. The Mbappe's also adopted an older boy called Jires Ekoko and had another boy called Ethan, both of whom would also play soccer for professional clubs.

The area where the Mbappes lived was called Bondy, in northeastern Paris. This area was plagued with social issues. It was known as a breeding ground for crime, terrorism, and anti-immigrant hate crimes. Riotous violence was a common occurrence.

Soccer provided an escape and a safe haven for young Kylian and other boys from the region. Kylian's earliest coaches remember him as a determined young boy who did everything better, faster, and more often than other players. His father had taught him the art of dribbling at an early age, and it seemed to give him an edge over the other boys. By the time he was approaching his teenage years, it was not uncommon for journalists and scouts to try to get contact details of Mbappe's coaches or his father (Smith & Peltier, 2018).

There was a little bit of a problem brewing, though. Young

players from Mbappe's area and background had gained a bad reputation, and many teams were reluctant to take on players like this. There were underlying prejudices based on racism, as most of these boys were descendants of African and Middle Eastern immigrants and of working class (or lower). The general feeling was Soccer in France, played by the working class; the working class means *banlieues* (the societal outskirts of Paris), and banlieues means thugs. The idea was that these players bond together and only bring trouble into the big clubs and even the French national team (Smith & Peltier, 2018). Some of these discriminated players don't even consider themselves French and refuse to take any national pride activities, like singing the national anthem.

For his part, Kylian always conducted himself in a mature and professional manner, even from a very young age. He got along well with players from all walks of life. Rich or poor, black or white, or anything in between, it didn't matter to Kylian. If you were on the soccer field, you were his friend.

The World at His Feet

Kylian Mbappe had already made a name for himself at Monaco and Paris Saint Germain within his first few seasons playing top-

Kylian Mbappe (1998 -)

flight soccer. He helped Monaco to win their first Ligue 1 title in 17 years and then Paris Saint-Germain to three successive titles. Most experts had agreed by the time the 2018 World Cup rolled around that he was head and shoulders above any other player in his age bracket and already one of the best players in the world. As a result, there were constant headlines in newspapers and chatter on online platforms.

"Mbappe to Real Madrid?"

"Manchester City to Break Transfer Record to Bring in Mbappe?"

For the time being, Mbappe was happy at Paris Saint-Germain and happy to stay put in France around the time of the World Cup. France entered the World Cup as one of the favorites. A generation had now passed since they had last won the World Cup. He was still only 19 years old and not quite the well-rounded player he would become, but Mbappe was already seen as an integral part of this French team.

France started the tournament with a bang, beating Australia 2-1 and then Peru 1-0. It was during this match against Peru that Mbappe scored his first of what would go on to become many World Cup goals. They drew their last match of the group stages to top their group.

They were come up against a star-studded Argentina team which included Lionel Messi, Angel Di Maria and Sergio Aguero. The French, however, were no slouches either. In a match worthy of having been a final, Mbappe scored twice in the second half. His two goals proved to be the difference, as France ran out 4-3 winners. France would go on to beat Uruguay in the quarterfinals and Belgium in the semifinals to set up a final showdown with Croatia.

Looking to emulate the great team of 1998 were a new breed of young and hungry players looking to write their names in the history books. None more so than Mbappe. A crowd of over 78,000 people packed into the stadium, and a nearby thunderstorm only added to the tension. Even all of this was not enough to break Mbappe's nerves of steel.

When the match finally got underway, it was Croatia who looked to be the stronger side. Luckily for France, Croatia couldn't capitalize on their great start. It was France who drew first blood when they went 1-0 up after Mario Mandzukic headered the ball into his own goal 19 minutes in. Croatia drew level 10 minutes later, but France went up a goal again when Antoine Griezmann converted a penalty at the 38-minute mark. This gave France a 2-1 lead going into the second half. Mbappe was 45 minutes away from glory.

Kylian Mbappe (1998 -)

The French attack did not slow down in the second half. Mbappe played an instrumental role in setting up France's third goal, which was to give them a two-goal cushion. With one hand already on the cup, Mbappe nailed a shot from 25 yards out that found the back of the net. It was not only a goal that would be talked about (and see young kids attempting to replicate) for years to come, but Mbappe also became the youngest player since Pele to score a goal in a World Cup final and only the second teenager.

While Croatia managed to score one more goal, France held on to win their first World Cup in 20 years! The whole of France rejoiced, and none louder than Mbappe's hometown! By being part of the World Cup-winning team, Mbappe had become the youngest player since Pele to do so. Not a bad comparison.

He would go on to become the second player ever to score a hat trick in our World Cup Final, in an unlucky loss to Argentina and teammate Lionel Messi. On the club level, he would continue to dominate, though, winning.

Reaching the Top and Bring Others Along

In 2017, Mbappe would often think back to his childhood years. He was so grateful that he was given the opportunity to get off the streets and not fall into the traps that so many of his peers had fallen into. He knew that without soccer, there was every possibility he would have fallen into those traps as well.

He had heard about a charity called *Premiers de Cordee*. It is a French expression and refers to a person who reaches the top and helps others do the same. To Mbappe, this spoke directly to him. He felt that he had just about reached the top, and he would like to give as many kids as possible the opportunity to do the same. The Premiers de Cordee specifically dealt with children who had extended hospital stays and/or had disabilities from the region that Mbappe grew up in.

He reached out to the charity and started arranging visits with some of these kids. As he arrived, children would run up to meet him, many with tears in their disbelieving eyes. Within minutes, though, they would be chatting with him like they've been lifelong friends. The progression from "I can't believe it's really you," "You are my hero," and "What's it like being the best soccer player in the world," to "Who's your favorite team to play

Kylian Mbappe (1998 -)

with on FIFA," would usually take a few minutes. He would also play ball with the kids and even show them some tricks. To many of these kids, he was simply a friend.

Before the 2018 World Cup, Mbappe started thinking about how he could make more of a difference in the lives of the kids from his native area. He came to the conclusion that if France were to win the World Cup, he would give all his winnings back to the kids.

After France won, Mbappe made good on his promise. He not only donated all $500,000 of his winnings to the Premiers de Cordee, but he also had (through his sponsors) a new, state-of-the-art futsal pitch installed in the community.

He continues to see himself as an example that being born in the *banlieues* does not have to mean you are destined to lead a terrible life. He also isn't ashamed of where he comes from. He still goes back regularly to his old school. Even buying tickets for the school kids to watch him play in the 2016 World Cup (Grez & Vandoome, 2018).

He is hopeful that this message of tolerance, courage and hope in the face of adversity, and in spite of diversities, will continue to spread beyond just the *banlieues* and Paris, but throughout France and the world. As of the end of 2023, there is no brighter star in the soccer world than Kylian Mbappe. Owing to all that he does on the field and the seemingly bigger role he plays off the field, it would not be hard to imagine him playing a much bigger role in French society one day. Perhaps even as Prime Minister...

Activities

1. Kylian Mbappe grew up playing with friends from all walks of life and different backgrounds. Do you have any friends or family who come from a different country, culture, religion, or background than your own? What are some things you have learned about their norms that are different from your own?

2. Kylian Mbappe saw great success at a very young age. Who are three of your favorite teenage sports stars? What do you enjoy about them?

3. Kylian Mbappe has been known to buy tickets for fans. Have you ever watched a live soccer match or live sport? If you have, what did you enjoy most about the experience? If you have not yet, what would you like to go watch and why?

Conclusion

Soccer is often said to be a universal language. It speaks volumes that so many children over the decades have found footballing heroes who probably don't even speak their language and might never have even heard of their cities or countries. It would not be uncommon to see children in the 1960's deepest, rural Africa run through the streets with a soccer ball, calling themselves Pele. Or to have Japanese boys in the early 2000s having their walls covered in David Beckham posters.

As we have seen in the above pages, there have been countless ways in which these popular soccer players have performed acts on- and off-the-field that has and will continue to inspire children. From those who took the sport to countries where it wasn't widely popular, those who would become presidents, the women who have and continue to pave the way for equality in the sport, those who have stopped wars, those who overcame great odds, and those who use their fame to continue to make the world a better place for others, soccer is filled with inspiring heroes.

For well over a century now, soccer has been the world's most widely played sport. Armed with the knowledge of this book, it is up to the children of today to decide how they can use the sport of soccer to change the world. It does not have to be as big as bringing the sport to a country—you can start by introducing it to your school friends. You don't have to use soccer to become the president of your country to make a difference—you can start by becoming a hall monitor. And you don't have to unite a country either—but perhaps soccer can bring your friends and people you don't always get along with together.

The power of soccer will continue to inspire young children for generations to come. The next Ronaldo, Messi, and Mbappe is already probably well on his way in a youth development system somewhere. And who knows? It could just be you...

Leave Your Feedback on Amazon

Please think about leaving some feedback via a review on Amazon. It may only take a moment, but it really does mean the world for small authors like myself :)

Even if you did not enjoy this title, please let me know the reason(s) in your review so that I may improve this title and serve you better.

From the Author

My mission with this series is to create practical and helpful parenting content that will not only help you maximize your child's potential, but also make your parenting journey as manageable as possible.

I hope that this book was able to help fulfill that mission and provide you with lots of value. Thank you for your purchase!

Don't forget your free gifts!

(My way of saying thank you for your support)

Simply visit **haydenfoxmedia.com** to receive the following:

- 10 Powerful Dinner Conversations To Create Amazing Kids

- 10 Magical Affirmations To Help Kids Become Unstoppable in Life

(you can also scan this QR code)

Printed in Great Britain
by Amazon

48382182R00086